"The genius of this book is that it takes a Biblical Christian Worldview in answering many profound and soul-searching questions about life and faith. It provides concise, straightforward and easy-to-understand responses based on God's Word, not politically correct cultural opinions. It will be an invaluable resource for America's youth, their parents, young adults and youth ministry leaders. It is a must-read for any person genuinely seeking God's truth for living a meaningful, purposeful and joyful life now and for eternity."

—**Michele Bachmann**, Author; International Speaker; Executive Director of Well Versed, Inc., Co-chair, Jerusalem Prayer Breakfast; Board Member, Family Research Council; Member US Congress for eight years, Presidential Candidate in 2012.

"It's no secret that Christianity seems to be losing ground in our culture, especially among young people in part, this may be because so much time is spent answering questions people are not asking, combined with not giving clear and straightforward answers to the questions they are asking. This book goes a long way towards addressing this issue head-on. Clear, concise and to the point, it is the perfect book to put into the hands of anyone seeking serious answers to serious questions about God, His character and His nature."

—**Robert Cathcart**, Executive Director, In His Steps Foundation

"In clear, precise, understandable language *Answers to Your Greatest Questions* provides a comprehensive picture of what it means to live the Christian life. It provides answers to the pressing questions of young people today."

—**David T. Dombrowiak**, President and CEO Community West Foundation to *Life's Greatest Questions* booklet to equip many of our staff in dealing with the issues of the day and to provide a place for youth to get answers to life's toughest questions. The *Answers to Your Greatest Questions* book takes everything to a more expanded level and provides Biblical answers to almost every aspect of life. I highly recommend being equipped with such a great resource."

—**Al Schierbaum**, Executive Director Fellowship of
Christian Athletes of Greater Nashville

"This book's FAQs are a great resource to begin spiritual conversations with our student athletes, especially for the spiritually curious. Its wide range of truth-based answers to the profound questions of life and faith make it a wonderful resource for spiritual growth and discipleship. It is a book every young adult and their parents should own and discuss."

—**Carl Schweisthal**, Area Director, Athletes-in-Action,
The Ohio State University

"I heartily recommend, *Answers to Your Greatest Questions*, for everyone: Christians, non-Christians, those of other faiths and even the nonreligious. The questions the book addresses are both timely and unique. The straightforward answers are clear, readable and understandable. I have personally used the 12 frequently asked questions contained in Chapter One very effectively in a variety of settings. They start engaging conversations. The book will be a great aid to your personal evangelism and your life's journey."

—**Scott Sommer**, Theological Development Coordinator,
Cru (Campus Crusade for Christ)

"It is an absolute fact that youth who leave the church do so because they do not have their questions answered or their doubts satisfied prior to high school graduation. Dedicated servants of Christ who are in a position to know have provided the *Answers to Your Greatest Questions* to fill this need. This book is a timely and necessary read for youth, parents and youth leaders. It should be a required resource for all youth ministries having the goal of producing youth with life-long commitments to the Christian faith."

—**G. Lee Southard, PhD**, author of *To Know With Certainty*

"If you've ever said, 'Hey, Google, who is...' or 'Alexa, what is...' this book invites readers to ask, 'Hey, Bible, what does God say about this?' *Answers to Your Greatest Questions* is a compilation of actual (and eternal) questions of the heart and the loving, unchanging answers offered in God's Word. It recognizes that the 'greatest story ever told' is shared best when we listen first."

—**Stacy Windahl**, co-author of *Beyond the Castle, A Guide to Discovering Your Happily Ever After*

ANSWERS TO **YOUR** GREATEST QUESTIONS

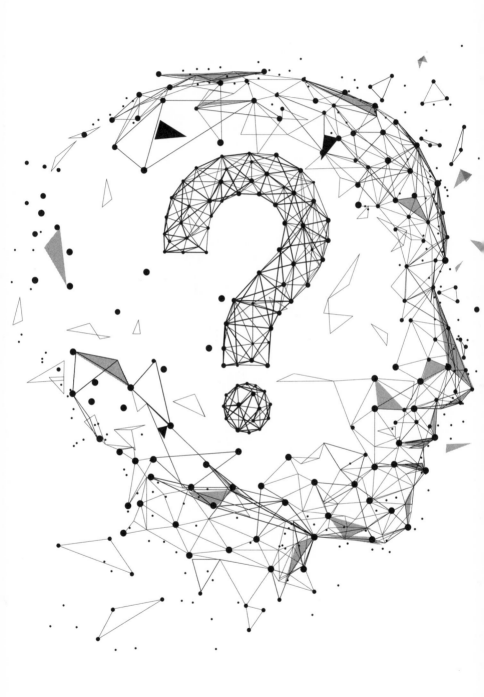

ANSWERS TO YOUR GREATEST QUESTIONS

A JOURNEY IN DISCOVERING GOD'S WISDOM

Living Dialog MINISTRIES | Be a new creation

Be a new creation

Answers to Your Greatest Questions: A Journey in Discovering God's Wisdom
© 2019 The Living Dialog Ministries (TLDM)
Published by The Living Dialog Ministries, Richmond, VA
www.livingdialog.org

ISBN: 978-0-9890791-1-2

18 17 16 15 14 13   7 6 5 4 3 2 1

Printed in the United States of America
Cover Design: Frank Gutbrod

To my wife of 57 years, Jean Marie, our two special sons David and Peter and their wonderful wives Suzanne and Ginger and to our four grandchildren Jack, Halley, Kate and Caroline.

TABLE OF CONTENTS

CHAPTER 7 SIN, REDEMPTION AND SALVATION 95

QUESTIONS ON SIN, REDEMPTION AND SALVATION

CHAPTER 11 CHRISTIANITY AND OTHER RELIGIONS 151
QUESTIONS ON CHRISTIANITY AND OTHER RELIGIONS

CHAPTER 12 GUIDE FOR CHRISTIAN LIVING 169
QUESTIONS ON A GUIDE FOR CHRISTIAN LIVING

FOREWORD — A LETTER TO READERS

Dear Reader:

I met Jack Dannemiller during the first week of a recent transitional pastorate, at a time in the life of one of his home churches when good leadership was needed. Jack did not come to tell me what to do or what I should be doing. He came to show me a bit of what he was doing and to share some resources that might be used by our church to reach out to a new generation for Christ.

In other words, he did not come to preach or criticize, but to help! Jack was often away during my time at his home church, but he was never disconnected. Each and every time he came to see me was a time of encouragement and inspiration. Jack is a positive person with a positive approach to problems, including spiritual problems. He is tireless in his efforts to make the Christian faith accessible to everyone.

Not everyone will agree with everything said in this book but they will be challenged to consider its wisdom and profound truths. What we can be absolutely sure of is that Jack is a person of integrity with a love for other human beings. He is reaching out as best he knows how to connect with a new generation for

Christ. We should all have his level of commitment, dedication, and willingness to share the Good News with others!

I heartily recommend that recipients of this book read and ponder its contents as well as the other books Jack has been so instrumental in publishing—and then put his ideas into practice as often as possible. God bless every reader.

Yours in Christ,

G. Christopher Scruggs

Reverend Dr. G. Christopher Scruggs practiced law in Houston, TX before responding to God's call to enter full-time ministry. As an attorney, he practiced corporate, securities, banking, and insurance law and has served on the boards of directors of a savings bank and non-profit. organizations over the years. In 1991, Chris left his law practice to attend seminary. More recently, he served as Of Counsel to a San Antonio law firm.

From 1994 through April 2017, Chris served in two pastorates near Memphis, Tennessee. He served for five years at First Presbyterian Church, Brownsville, TN and eighteen years at Advent Presbyterian Church, Cordova, TN. Most recently, Chris served as Team Coach, Session Moderator, and Transitional Pastor of Bay Presbyterian Church in Bay Village, Ohio from October 2017 through February 2019.

Chris is the author of *Centered Living/Centered Leading: The Way of Light and Love* (2010), *Path of Life: Wisdom Literature for Christ-Followers* (2014), and *Salt & Light: Everyday Discipleship* (2016). He and his wife, Kathy, wrote the *Salt & Light* study together. He is currently writing a book on discipleship.

Chris received his Master of Divinity from Union Theological Seminary in Richmond, Virginia., and his Doctor of Ministry degree from Asbury Theological Seminary in Wilmore, Kentucky. He also has a B.A. in Philosophy from Trinity University in San Antonio, Texas and a J.D. Degree from the University of Texas Law School in Austin. He is licensed to practice law in Texas.

PREFACE

Five years ago we created the highly successful booklet, *Answers to Life's Greatest Questions*. Tens of thousands have been published. Since then we have received many more of your questions. It's time to reveal the secrets of those questions and answers for you to ponder and enjoy. This new book is really all about your questions. Questions you've asked or would like to have asked and questions to which you are still seeking better, more understandable and truthful answers. Questions about creation. Questions about the meaning and purpose of life. Questions about life and death itself. Questions about heaven and hell and what happens when we die. Physical death, like taxes, is inescapable. Everyone eventually dies. Life has many options but eternity only two. What are those? This book has answers that will surprise you. Answers that will challenge you and expand your thinking. Answers about what really matters in life and in eternity. Answers that will take you on an adventure that will have you pondering the content for weeks and even years to come. Answers that will truly be life transforming. Answers that will shape your worldview. The introduction that follows will be your guide for your adventure through the 12 chapters in this book. So, fasten your "mental seatbelt" and take off on your journey of discovery, then visit us online at *www.LifesBasicQuestions.com* to download suggestions on how to use this book for evangelism, personal and family devotions or small group study.

INTRODUCTION

Welcome to the *Answers* book. This is the most comprehensive yet easy to understand answers book ever compiled. Our surveys of people of all ages has shown that the questions in this book are those that are top of mind for the curious, inquisitive, seekers of truth and even for Christian believers. It is designed for a journey in discovery. Discovery of answers to the profound questions of life that men and women have sought since the beginning of time: What is the meaning of life? What happens when I die? Does God really exist? Did God create life? Is God still involved in his creation today? Is the Bible unique among all other books?

Three thousand years ago the Greeks were known for pursuing answers to these age-old questions. Socrates became famous for his inquiry method of asking and answering questions known today as the Socratic method. Curiosity is one of the defining traits of all human nature. Young children frequently drive their parents to the brink by constantly asking questions, especially the question of "Why"? As people mature and experience life, the questions continue. Why does life hurt so much? What is man's noble purpose? Is heaven for real? Is there really such a state as eternal life? What is a Christian worldview?

Two thousand years ago a person appeared on the scene who also asked and answered many of these core questions of life. What was unique about his teaching and his answers was that those who listened recognized that he spoke with authority. They had not seen this type of profound wisdom in any other person who had wrestled with these most basic questions. Even King Solomon, who was generally recognized as the wisest person who ever lived, did not possess the wisdom that was exhibited in this individual. That person was Jesus Christ. His authority and understanding of the human condition came directly from God, the Creator of life.

Jesus' birth, teachings, miracles, prophecies, death, resurrection and ascension into Heaven affirmed his authority as the source of truthful answers to all questions of life. He was in fact who he claimed to be...the Son of God, Emmanuel, God with us! Therefore, the answers to the questions contained in this book come directly from the source of all knowledge and wisdom and truth, God's Word, the Bible, as revealed by the Holy Spirit to the members of the Living Dialogue Ministries answers team.

You may also be seeking understanding about some of the promises, mysteries and prophecies of the Bible. You will find that many of those topics are addressed in this book. On the other hand, you may want to know what God has to say about 21st-century cultural issues that impact human behavior and relationships; i.e., traditional marriage, truth and tolerance. Or, you might want to know the biblical worldview of creation, evolution, sin, heaven, hell and end-times events. These topics and more are addressed in the book's 12 chapters.

Introduction

It is our hope that on this journey of discovery you will find answers to many of your own life questions. Blaise Pascal, the brilliant mathematician, physicist, writer and theologian of the 17th century took this journey before you and discovered that "There is a God placed vacuum in the human soul that only God can fill." God knew that he alone could satisfy the longings of the human heart. May God reveal himself and his truth to you and satisfy your curiosity about life as you explore this book. Enjoy, and may God bless you.

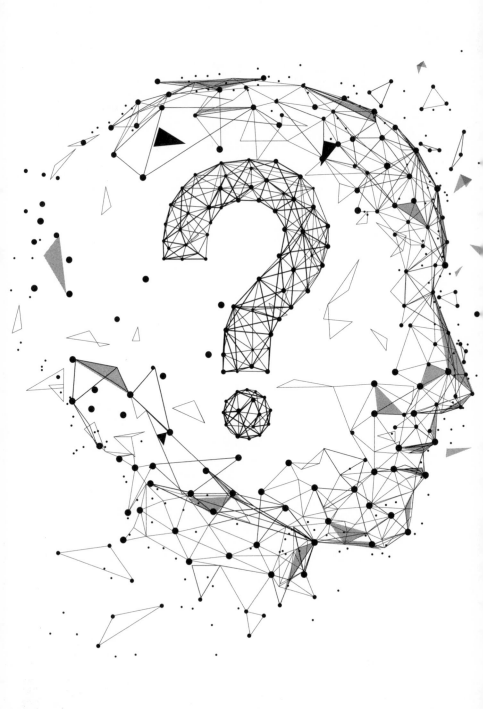

CHAPTER 1

MOST FREQUENTLY ASKED QUESTIONS

These 12 most Frequently Asked Questions were taken from surveys of church pastors, leaders of Christian Ministries like FCA, Young Life, Athletes-In-Action, CRU (Campus Crusade) and chaplains of professional and college sports teams regarding life and faith issues.

Those surveys pointed to the most important question which is, How does one become a Christian and gain eternal life? And then, the logical follow-on question: What are the next steps in the Christian life journey?

You will discover the answers to both of these at the end of this chapter. You might be amazed at how simply God has fashioned the truth that will set you free to be all that God created you to be from before you were born and how exciting it will be to pursue life with real meaning, purpose and passion.

"For God so loved the world that he gave his one and only Son, that whoever believes in him shall not perish but have eternal life." —John 3:16 (NIV)

MOST FREQUENTLY ASKED QUESTIONS

Q1 DOES GOD EXIST?

The short answer to this question is, "Yes, God exists". While no one has ever seen God, He has made Himself known to us. His existence is seen in His power and in His divine nature expressed in creation (Romans 1:20). The beauty and intricacy of this world speaks to the existence of God as creator. All that exists works to maintain the enormous machinery of our universe functioning in perfect harmony. You don't see God but you know He exists because of the harmony which He maintains.

As an example, consider this: you have never *seen* the wind. However, you can see its effects as it causes the gentle rippling of the grass and the sway of the branches of the trees. The movement of the air cannot be seen but we are definitely aware of its existence. Everyday you and I trust in things that we cannot or do not see yet we seldom question their existence. The counter question is then "Why do we believe in the existence of some things we cannot see but question God's existence simply because we cannot see Him with our physical eyes?"

There is a similarity to this observation of effect in the way that God moves and works among those who believe in Him. In John's gospel, we read that Christ appeared to His disciples after His resurrection. All of His disciples were present except for Thomas. When Thomas heard from the other disciples that Christ was risen, he stated *"Unless I see the nail marks in his hands and put my finger where the nails were, and put my hand into his side, I will not believe" (John 20:25 ESV)*. A week later, Christ appeared again to His disciples. This time Thomas was among them. Christ invited Thomas to feel the nail prints in His hands and for Thomas to place his hand into His side. Christ said, "Stop doubting and believe". It is interesting that, when confronted with the presence of Christ, Thomas required no such physical verification, rather he fell to his knees and proclaimed, "My Lord and my God!". To which Christ replied, *"Because you have seen me, you have believed; blessed are those who have not seen and yet have believed."*

This believing without visible evidence is called "faith" and it is vital for our Christian life (Hebrews 11:6). It is vital because God never makes the slightest attempt to explain Himself or His existence. The Bible begins with the words, *"In the beginning, God..." (Genesis 1:1)* and from that point forward, God's existence is an undefined assumption. He simply "is".

So, yes, God is real. He does exist. Even though you do not see Him with your physical eyes you still see His effects and influences on the world around us and you and I feel His presence. However, "experiencing His existence, His reality" requires faith. "Keep on asking, and you will receive what you ask for. Keep on seeking, and you will find. Keep on knocking, and the door will be opened to you." (Matthew 7:7 NLT).

Q2 WHAT IS GOD LIKE?

We can never fully understand God. His own Word tells us that we cannot understand Him. Psalm 145:3 tells us "Great is the Lord and greatly to be praised; and His greatness is unsearchable." However, we have glimpses and hints of what he is like. The creation speaks of his creative power and glory. Just look at sunrises and sunsets. The macro and micro worlds are beyond our understanding. The human body is such a marvelous creation that science and medicine will forever be trying to comprehend its complexity. Human love is impossible to fully grasp. Yet, greater still is the love that God has displayed throughout eternity. You and I need LOVE which really means that we need God. The Bible tells us that "God is love" (1 John 4:8). When understanding "what is God like?" we could begin with His love because it is more than what He is like, it is what He IS.

That said, here are some ideas of what God is like. He is eternal. He is personal; you can get to know him. He is one; unique—no other gods exist except him. He is spirit; he can be everywhere all the time. He is just; his justice is perfect. He is sovereign; he has absolute reign over every aspect of his creation. His is omnipotent; his power is unequaled throughout the universe. He is the source of all love, joy, beauty and wisdom.

That is why God is worthy of our worship our praise, our love and our obedience.

Q3 WHAT IS THE MEANING AND PURPOSE OF LIFE?

We are called to have a relationship with our Creator through faith and reliance on Jesus' sacrifice for us. It sounds simple because it is simple; just believe in Jesus Christ (Romans 10: 9) and rely on His Holy Spirit to live inside each of us, transforming us into the people that God created us to be (Romans 12:2).

We like to make it more complicated, but when Jesus Christ was asked point blank what the most important commandment was, He replied: "'Love the Lord your God with all your heart and with all your soul and with all your mind.' This is the first and greatest commandment. And the second is like it: 'Love your neighbor as yourself'" Matthew 22:36-40 (NIV).

Placing our faith in Christ's work on the cross and humbly yielding to Him will put us in right relationship with God.

That's the same relationship that Adam and Eve enjoyed before their sin severed that relationship. We are to walk as Christ would walk and represent him to others that are in our sphere of influence. Micah 6:8 says we are "... To act justly and to love mercy and to walk humbly with your God."

Q4 IF GOD EXISTS, WHY DOES LIFE HURT SO MUCH?

This life is not fair and it hurts. When this life hurts, we can draw upon God for comfort and love. We are all imperfect people who, out of God's love for us, are given the freedom to make choices. When we make choices out of selfishness, pride, anger, fear or any other negative emotion or motive, we hurt others, but even more, we hurt ourselves. This is sin, or missing the best that God desires for us. It started with Adam and Eve disobeying God in the Garden of Eden (Genesis 3). Since the moment that sin entered the world, it seems that all of our lives are full of trouble and sorrow (Job 14:1). The good news is that God has a plan through which our lives can be full of joy and fulfillment in spite of the pains of life (1 Peter 1:7-8).

You see, God can use anything, even evil, done to us for our own good (Romans 8:28). God cares about our character, our heart and the eternal destiny of our souls more than anything, and He allows us to go through hurt and pain so that we can grow and mature. We can thank God that He is just, and is not fair with us, because if he was fair, he would reject us because we fall so far short of the standard he has set for us. We have failed, and by our actions we have separated ourselves from God. But God has created for us a pathway to reconciliation through Christ's work on the cross (2 Corinthians 5:21).

But even though we have given up on God, he hasn't given up on us. Out of His love for us, God sent His only son, who was perfect and without sin, to Earth to take upon himself the sins of everyone—past, present and future—so that we can enjoy a life in relationship to him (Isaiah 53:6). Jesus dying in our place was unfair, but necessary, for God's best for all of us.

Q5 WHAT HAPPENS WHEN I DIE?

As Christians, the Bible tells us that, just as God is made up of three parts (Father, Son, Holy Spirit), we are also made up of three parts: soul, spirit and body. While it is still a big mystery as to what exactly happens when we die, science and personal anecdotes corroborate the truth that our soul separates from our earthly body (2 Cor. 5:6-8). Science has proven that there is a difference in weight of 21 grams after people have died, indicating that the soul actually has mass. There have also been a few personal anecdotes of dead people coming back to life. Even though each relates somewhat different experiences, there are enough similarities between them to corroborate each other. It's great to have evidence to back up the Bible, but ultimately life after death is a matter of faith in God's Word.

Death itself is the result of Adam and Eve's disobedience in the Garden of Eden, but because of Jesus, we have a chance to live again (1 Corinthians. 15:22). After our earthly death, our souls continue on in life (with God in Heaven: John 3:16) or death (eternal torment and separation from God in hell: Revelation 20:15). The decisions we make during our lifetime, right up until we take our final breath, determines where our souls go at death. The humble criminal who was crucified next to Jesus made just such a decision while hanging on the cross and was saved from an eternity in hell (Luke 23:43).

If we have faith in Jesus when He says, "I am the resurrection and the life. The one who believes in me will live, even though they die; and whoever lives by believing in me will never die." (John 11:25,26) then our souls will continue to live with Christ in heaven. If we pridefully disregard the sacrifice that Jesus gave for us all, then we will "pay the penalty of eternal destruction, away from the presence of the Lord and from the glory of his power" (2 Thessalonians. 1:9). It's not that God wants to punish us like this (2 Peter 3: 9). In fact, God has given us the ability to choose our own destiny. In life there are many choices, but for eternity only two. You must make a choice.

Ultimately, physical death is not the end of our existence. Our souls will continue to exist for all eternity, either in Heaven in God's presence or in hell, cut off from Him forever. The choice of where and how we exist after our bodies die is our own.

Q6 IS SIN REALLY SERIOUS?

You bet! All sin separates. It causes a gulf between man and God and between man and man (Isaiah 59:2). Sin is so serious and causes such a huge separation from God that the only remedy is for God the Father to send His Son into this world to die in our place in order to reconcile mankind to Himself (2 Corinthians 5: 18).

All sin is very serious and has serious consequences. Many people associate sin exclusively with the Ten Commandments (Exodus 20: 1-17). The problem arises when we fail to understand that the Ten Commandments actually identify God's view of sin in relation to His own holiness. The commandments point out just how sinful human nature really is and how far we are from God's holy nature (Romans 3:20).

We find a common definition of sin in Merriam-Webster's dictionary as, "an action that is or is felt to be highly reprehensible; an offense or a fault; an offense against a religious or moral law."

"Sin will take you farther than you want to go, keep you longer than you want to stay, and cost you more than you want to pay. —" Ravi Zacharaias, an author and Christian apologist once said. In 1 John 3:4 the Bible says that sin is the practicing of disobedience and the breaking of God's law. In the Bible, sin also literally means to "miss the mark". So we see that sin may not only be a single act, it can become a choice of lifestyle like in the term "living in sin". Once a person gives way to temptation and sins, the next sin can become easier to justify in a person's mind. What is really serious is that unconfessed sin and failure to repent or turn away from sinful habits ultimately leads to both physical and spiritual (eternal) death (James 1: 13-15).

All sin eventually destroys everything that it touches. There are innumerable stories of men and women, great and small, who learned just how damaging the consequences of their sin can be. Just watch the nightly news and you can see it in real time.

The good news is that God has provided a way for us to overcome our sinful human nature (John 1: 10-12). The solution is found in acknowledging that Jesus took our place on the cross to pay the penalty for our sin, asking for forgiveness and then allowing Jesus to turn our hearts and minds away from our sinful desires and towards his love, beauty and friendship (John 3: 14-18).

Q7 WHY WOULD ANYONE WANT TO FOLLOW JESUS?

Life is about choices. Decisions we make have outcomes that impact our lives, influence our behaviors, our beliefs and our relationships with others. We can choose to continue with business as usual, enjoying success based on the standards defined by our secular culture. Or, we can take an honest look at Jesus of the Bible and dare to ask what the consequences might be if we really believed, trusted and obeyed him. Would following Jesus really bring life meaning and purpose, joy and peace and eternal life? The fact is that each and every day, for over 2000 years, people around the world from every nation choose to follow Jesus who gave His life and was raised from the dead so that all who follow him can enjoy God's kingdom, peace with God and everlasting life. Jesus proved that He was God by signs, miracles, profound wisdom, and overcoming death and the grave. In John 14:6 we read Jesus' own confirmation that He is the only way to heaven and eternal life when He said, "I am the way and the truth and the life. No one comes to the Father except through me." So the question really is, *"Why wouldn't everyone want to follow Jesus?"* Life is a gift from God. It can only be lived to the fullest in a relationship with Jesus. Remember, happiness depends on happenings which are temporary, but real joy and fulfillment, which are eternal, are only found in Jesus. That is why untold millions have chosen to follow him.

Q8 IF I'M GOOD, DO I GET TO GO TO HEAVEN?

We can never be good enough to enter Heaven on our own merit (Isaiah 64:6). The apostle Paul reminds us that "all have sinned and fall short of the glory of God" (Romans 3:23), and that salvation from this sin is costly, but freely given to us (Romans 6:23). Jesus carried our sins to the cross and died so that we might have life. That great sacrifice is spelled out in John 3:16 "For God so loved the world that he gave his one and only Son, that whoever believes in him shall not perish but have eternal life."

We're not saying that doing good isn't important. To the contrary, the Bible writers repeatedly offer guidance and direction for living in a manner that honors God and serves his creation. Works, those good things you do, through faith, are good and profitable for all people (Titus 3:8), but it is only through faith in Christ Jesus (John 14:16) and His sacrifice for us that we are saved, not by our works, otherwise we might think too highly of ourselves and devalue Jesus and His life. Faith is what saves, but as James writes in chapter 2 of his letter, "faith without works is dead." Read the context in which this is written in James 2:20-24. Works are the fruit of our faith and obediently done for the glory of God. ". . . let your light shine before others, that they may see your good deeds and glorify your Father in heaven" Matthew 5:16.

Your salvation and eternity in heaven are not free. But, since you could not purchase them for yourself, they were purchased for you through Christ's sacrificial death on the cross. You receive them by simply believing that Christ died for your sins, asking for His forgiveness and then receiving them freely. So, in essence, we "are good", that is, we do things that are good and abstain from doing things that are bad because we **are** saved, not in order to **be** saved.

Q9 HOW CAN A LOVING GOD CONDEMN ANYONE TO HELL?

God doesn't send anyone to hell. People choose to go there when they reject Jesus Christ. Surprised by that answer? You shouldn't be. God is both loving and just. He won't force anyone to love him. In fact, he allows everyone to pursue the longings of their lives. People who want nothing to do with God in this life will be granted that desire for eternity. That results in eternal separation from God who is the source of all love, joy and beauty. But God's desire is for all of us to enjoy him. He wants everyone to be saved from the torments of an endless pursuit of that which will never truly satisfy—an eternity devoid of love and beauty (see 2 Peter 3:9). He has provided a way for us to enjoy a much better eternal life, one in which there is no more sadness or disappointment or loneliness or war or pestilence or pain or death. It comes through a personal relationship with his son, Jesus Christ. God is patient and long-suffering, but eventually all must choose. When we die, we will meet God the Creator face-to-face. There is no reincarnation. There are no second chances. When we die, we may discover that our choices in life lead to an eternity in hell. Choose wisely.

Q10 DID JESUS REALLY COME BACK FROM THE DEAD?

Few historical events have been as heatedly contested and debated as the resurrection of Christ. Even so, very few historical events are as well documented as Christ rising from the dead. From the historical accounts of the gospels to the archeological evidence that continues to confirm the Biblical account of Christ's appearances after his crucifixion, there are few, if any, events from over 1000 years ago that are so firmly established as fact as the resurrection of Jesus Christ. Historians who were non-believers confirm that Christ's body was missing from the tomb after His crucifixion. Historians who were neutral non-believers recount the testimony of countless witnesses who physically saw Jesus after He emerged from the grave.

From the scriptures we learn that, within hours of His resurrection, several of the women who followed Jesus either encountered Jesus personally or saw the empty tomb and were instructed by angels to go and tell His disciples (John 20 and Matthew 28). We read that all 11 apostles saw Jesus within days of His return from the dead (Luke 24: 36-49). Over 100 disciples witnessed His ascension into Heaven (Acts 1: 4-11). Paul states that over 500 people witnessed the living, risen Christ (1 Corinthians 15: 5-8).

Had Jesus not been resurrected, His enemies would have produced a body and quashed the whole story. The Roman soldiers who were assigned the duty of guarding the tomb risked execution for failing in their duties had they let Jesus' disciples steal the body. In the first century Jewish culture, women had little credibility, yet it was they who first discovered the empty tomb and their reports have been preserved for two millennia. This evidence helps us believe that Jesus came back from the dead, but we are called upon today to believe without having witnessed the physical Jesus. John, one of Jesus' closest disciples reminds us that Jesus himself taught that we can enjoy a certain blessing that comes from believing without seeing (John 20:29). Christians believe that after being crucified and pronounced dead, Jesus, the Son of God was resurrected and ascended into heaven, after which he sent the Holy Spirit to guide our lives. God has given us the freedom to believe, or not; to accept his sacrifice on the cross or not. But, with evidence so overwhelming, what do you believe?

Q11 HOW DOES ONE BECOME A CHRISTIAN?

Becoming a Christian isn't about going to church, and it isn't just about changing how you live. Becoming a Christian is all about allowing God to change our hearts and our character. The Bible tells us that "... God looks at the heart" of a person (1 Samuel 16: 7). So, becoming a Christian involves an inward change that begins when you believe in your heart and confess with your mouth that Jesus is Lord, and that Jesus was raised from the dead after he sacrificed himself on the cross, thereby paying the penalty for your sins (Romans 10:8-11). Jesus waits for our invitation and for our heart to be open to his love (Revelation 3: 20).

Maybe you went to church when you were younger, but never accepted Jesus as your Savior. Maybe you've been living your life your own way and have never taken into account what it takes to live differently.

It's never too late to become saved by grace and to live life walking with Jesus, even at the end of your life (2 Corinthians 6: 2). God responds to humility, just look at the humble criminal on the cross who was crucified alongside Jesus (Luke 23:39-43). Even though this man had lived a selfish life, harming himself and others, in the end he took an honest look at his actions, saw the results of his selfishness and the justness of his death. But, in Jesus, he saw an innocent man being unjustly killed.

In that moment, the criminal recognized Jesus as the Son of God and Jesus recognized the repentant heart of a criminal and welcomed him into the family of God.

In Luke 23:42-43, we read, "Then he said, "Jesus, remember me when you come into your kingdom." Jesus answered him, "Truly I tell you, today you will be with me in paradise." In this scripture we find the way of salvation, the way to become a Christian. We find HOPE. In these verses we find Jesus Christ, the only way to eternal life (John 14:6).

Q12 WHAT ARE THE NEXT STEPS IN THE CHRISTIAN LIFE JOURNEY?

Every journey begins with a single step. If you have admitted to God that you are a sinner in need of a savior and asked for his forgiveness for your sinful life, you have already taken the first step. Repenting of your old ways, which means turning to follow Jesus, is the second step. It is also important to share this exciting news! Tell your family, friends, and everyone you encounter. Shout it out to the world! Part of the Christian life is doing what others have done for over 2000 years by spreading the good news of Jesus Christ with those you meet. You could also go to social networking sites to share your new life in Christ with others or even to help those struggling with life's challenges.

But, keep in mind that you will get pushback. The devil will try to deceive you—make you doubt that becoming a Christian was a wise decision. So be prepared. Recognize that the road ahead may not be smooth. There will be bumps and obstacles along the way. Like everyone else, you have a lifetime of experiences, of regrets, of trying to control your life. It will take time to put them in your past. You will certainly encounter those who will try to influence and challenge your faith or may not want you to enjoy the fullness of life that comes from a relationship with Jesus Christ. God will give you the courage to stand strong. Just ask him. Always remember that you are not alone. When you accept Jesus as Lord and Savior you are promised a special gift. That gift is the Holy Spirit of God that comes into your life to direct your thoughts and actions in your journey with Jesus. He will guide you to all truth and enable you to develop a Biblical worldview as you study God's inspired scriptures, the Bible. Read your Bible daily and often and start with the book of John to get a first-hand account of the life of Jesus Christ. And, find a church which is founded on God's Word, the Bible and where the Bible is taught on a regular basis. Attend that church and fellowship regularly and often and find the strength that can only be found in a family of believers who, like you, have left behind a life lived according to their own whims and desires and have fully committed their lives to Christ, to His ways and to His plan.

For some, these steps may seem simplistic and formulaic. For others they may seem to be a great sacrifice. But once you have found Christ, these steps will help assure that your faith remains strong and that you find the fullness of life and joy that God surely has planned for you.

"And I am sure of this, that he who began a good work in you will bring it to completion at the day of Jesus Christ," said the Apostle Paul to the Church in Phillippi.

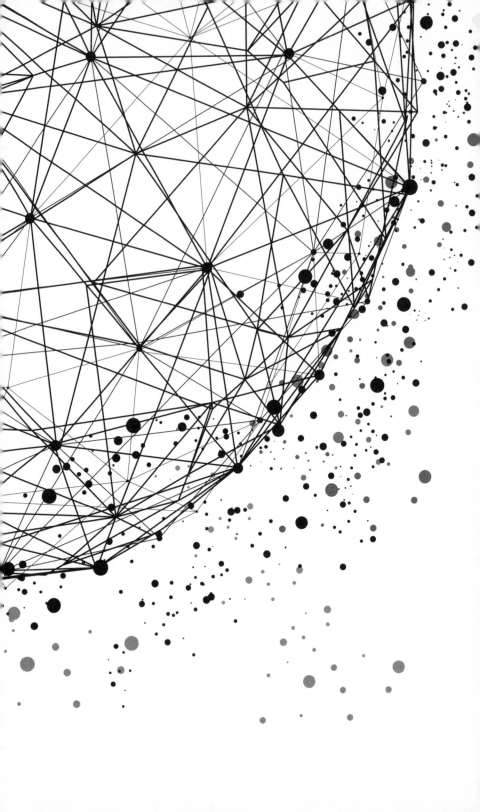

CHAPTER 2

GOD — CREATOR, INTELLIGENT DESIGNER

In ages past, before the beginning of time, GOD! God is eternal, He is the great I AM! God is the embodiment of all wisdom, knowledge and power. God is the intelligent designer of all that there is or ever will be. He speaks and it happens. God is triune in nature; Father, Son and Holy Spirit. God has revealed himself in creation, in scripture and in Jesus Christ. God is sovereign over all creatures great and small including man and woman. In this chapter we answer just nine unique questions about God. We have barely scratched the surface of what God is like. There would not be enough space in all the libraries on Earth to answer all the questions about God. Hopefully you will get a few new insights into God's character and come to love him, serve him, and obey him. He wants to have a relationship with you just like he had with Adam before Adam sinned. After all, you were created in God's image and he loves you!

QUESTIONS CONCERNING GOD

Q1 WHERE IS GOD?

Everybody asks this and the answer is actually simple and direct. He is here, right now no matter where you are or what you are doing. It's referred to as being **omnipresent**. God's Spirit is present everywhere throughout creation. In his great power and knowledge God created the heavens and the earth (Genesis 1:1). That means He existed before the creation of the universe and thus, all space, time and matter that was created when our universe was created. This means that God transcends these dimensions, not being limited by them but over them. Because he transcends what he created, God operates in and out of them at any time and any place in anyway he wills. He is not in just one place. When Moses inquired of God who God was, God's answer was simple "I Am" (Exodus 3:13-14). Jesus gave the same answer (John 8: 58). "I Am" means God was, is and always will be. No one else can say that. When Jesus physically left this Earth He had promised that He would send the Holy Spirit, the third part of the triune God to be with us and he did. Being spiritual, the Holy Spirit is not limited by space, time and matter. Thus God is everywhere, all the time as the Holy Spirit. God literally is with you. When you pray you are talking to God but do not envision that your prayer is going up to some far away palace with a bearded old man sitting on a throne. No you are face to face with God through the Holy Spirit whose purpose is to intercede on your behalf with God (Rom 8:26,27). Through prayer you can draw even closer to God, so close that God is in you.

(Text provided by, G. Lee Southard, Ph.D Author, *To Know With Certainty*)

Q2 WHAT DOES THE SOVEREIGNTY OF GOD MEAN?

According to the Bible, all things—past, present, and future—are ruled by God and are under his power and control. God rules according to his eternal purpose which includes his creation, human history and redemption of mankind (Isaiah 46: 9-10). Sovereignty of God can also be described in three big words: **omnipotence,** which means all powerful (Jeremiah 32:26); **omniscient** (Psalm 147:5), which means all knowing; and **omnipresent**, which means he is everywhere at once working continuously to accomplish his will (Psalm 139: 7-10). Since God is all powerful and knows everything, including our thoughts and needs, and since he is everywhere at the same time, you can enjoy peace knowing that a Sovereign God is involved with his creation, including you (Psalm 103:19).

Q3 DOES GOD HAVE A PERSONALITY?

Yes. In his book, *The Great Doctrines of the Bible*, William Evans presents this compelling argument:

> "It is best to define personality when used of the Divine Being or God very carefully and not by human standards. God was not made in the image of man. God is not a deified man. Only God the Father has a perfect personality. When one possesses the attributes and qualities of personality, then personality may be unquestionably predicted of such a being."

All the names of God imply personality. When Moses asked God "who should I say is sending me", God said, "say that, 'I Am', has sent you" (Exodus 3:14). The central idea of this name is both existence and personality. As you search the Scriptures you will find that God grieves, gets angry, can be jealous, loves and even hates. In addition, he cares, provides, disciplines, forgives, heals, listens and much more. Finally, personality exists where there is intelligence, mind, will, reason, individuality, self-consciousness and self-determination or free will. So, it is fair to say that both God and man have personalities so they can have communion and personal relationships (Psalm 8: 4-6). Christianity is unique in that a human being can have an intimate personal relationship with an infinite, eternal and omniscient divine being, God, who created all that exists in the heavens and on the earth. That's amazing!

Q4 HOW CAN A PERSON CONNECT WITH GOD?

Connecting with God is easier than one might think. Why? Because God promises to reveal himself to everyone that honestly and diligently seek him (Luke 7:7). First, however, you must believe that God exists. You need to look no further than the creation which acknowledges that God is the creator and designer of all that exist including human life. Since creation, God's invisible qualities—his eternal power and divine nature— have been clearly seen. The creation reflects God's character, wisdom, sovereignty and unconditional love. The next connecting link to God is the Bible. God speaks to most people through his living word, the Bible. So, get a Life Application Bible in modern translation like the New International Version (NIV) and start reading in the New Testament with the Gospel of John. You will definitely encounter and connect with God as you read the chapters and verses. Be sure to pay close attention to the footnotes.

As you encounter Jesus in John's Gospel, decide to put your faith and trust in him as both Savior and Lord. Why? Jesus is the key to your connection to God and to both a meaningful life and to eternal life. Jesus said,

> "I am the way, the truth and the life. No one comes to God the Father except through me." John 14:6

His words here are both exclusive and all inclusive. That actually keeps things clear and simple. It is only Jesus and no one else. Finally, have a quiet time of prayer each day with the Lord sharing your life and listening for God's responses. When you practice these activities regularly you will get connected to God. Guaranteed! Then share what God has revealed to you with others. You will be empowered to love your neighbor as yourself with that unconditional love that God alone provides.

Q5 WHAT DOES IT MEAN TO BE CREATED IN THE IMAGE OF GOD?

First, it does not mean that we look like him, which the word image implies in the English language. God is Spirit and the few times in scripture where he was present (other than when he came and lived among us as Jesus), he was not able to be looked at. The Hebrew word translated as image into English, like many ancient Hebrew words, has multiple meanings. It can refer to all our spiritual and personal characteristics or attributes. The question might be rephrased or clarified to ask,

"With which attributes of God's have humans been endowed?" Here are just a few of those attributes:

- *Spirit or Soul* — An eternal nature, created to live forever (Genesis 2:7).
- *Free Will* — The right to choose, an ability to trust or reject God (Mark 8:34).
- *Conscience* — Knowing right and wrong, distinguishing good from evil (Joshua 24:15).
- *Mind* — Capacity to think, reason, discern, understand, etc. (Isaiah 1: 18).
- *Curiosity* — Seeking truth, discovering God, the how/why questions (Proverbs 8:17).
- *Design Intuition* — Knowing instinctively by observation and experience.
- *Heart* — Your personality traits, love, courage, compassion, ambition, etc., "Tender Hearted or Hard Hearted".
- *Creativity* — Art, music, science, writing, designing, building, medicine and much more (Psalm 19: 1-6).

It is these very personal attributes that enable us to meet and talk to God in our prayers and devotions. It is this nature that enables God to hear and respond according to his perfect will. He is not some distant and impersonal deity but an ever-present loving heavenly father. It is often said that if you want to hear God talk to you, read the Bible aloud. Being created in God's image matters because it is the essence of having a meaningful and purposeful life now and forever. Christianity is unique in that we have a God with whom we can have that deeply personal and intimate contact both now and throughout all eternity. Because of His nature and the fact that we are made in his image, we can enjoy a loving relationship with God. But that relationship is only possible through trust in Jesus Christ as Lord and Savior. That's Grace! How great that is and how great is God (Philippians 3: 1-7).

Q6 CAN YOU KNOW GOD PERSONALLY?

The answer is yes. In the beginning Adam walked and talked and fellowshipped with God every day. That was how God intended life to be for every person ever born; to actually know God personally. Unfortunately, Adam sinned when he disobeyed God's one and only rule. Sin then separated man from God. The "good news" is that placing one's trust in Jesus as Savior and Lord restores that relationship so a person can actually know God personally. God has a wonderful, exciting plan for everyone's life. Life's greatest adventure is discovering that plan and living it to the 'Max'. There is only one way to God. There is no path as some religions claim. Jesus said, "I am the way, the truth and the life. No one comes to the Father (God) except through me" (John 14:6).

God is a personal God. He desires relationships with His creation (2 Corinthians 5: 18-20). He has given man the free will to say I want to know you or I don't. The choice is personal. The choice is ours. The choice is yours. Choose wisely.

Q7 DOES GOD STILL SPEAK TO US?

In the Bible, there are many times where God personally interacted with humans. In addition to Adam and Eve, he spoke to Noah, Moses, Elijah, Jeremiah, Daniel and John the Baptist to name but a few. He wrestled with Jacob. Yes, God speaks to us in many different ways (Job 33:14), by an audible voice, as with Jeremiah when he called him while he was sleeping. He also speaks through visions and dreams, but the most common way is through his written word, the Bible (Romans 10:17). Helping us to understand what the Bible is saying is one of the roles of the Holy Spirit who helps us gain understanding and wisdom and helps us see how a particular scripture applies to our current situation and life. God still speaks (John 8:47). We who are saved have the Holy Spirit living inside of us so that we can enjoy an even more intimate relationship with Him (John 16:13).

Q8 HOW DOES A PERSON GET RIGHT WITH GOD?

Who would not want to be 'right' with our creator, right? Again, the short answer is you can never "get right" with God by yourself. That's right, you can never be good enough, never be sinless enough nor can you follow God's words so perfectly that you can make yourself "right with God" (Philippians 3: 3-9). God, the Father is perfectly holy and any sign of sin is not acceptable to him, no matter how small, how large, or in our present or our past. But, the most wonderful thing has happened. He loved us so much He provided a Savior, His only son, for you and for me (1 John 1: 8-9). We can never fully understand or comprehend the indescribable love He has for us, but we can experience it. The Savior, Jesus Christ, led a perfectly holy sinless life, He suffered and was brutally killed. Then, His perfect life was accepted by the Father and

He rose from the dead and ascended into heaven with God the Father. Now God chooses to see us even with all our sins and imperfections through Christ and we, through faith in Christ, are now 'Right with God'.

This faith is called salvation—saved from being slaves to sin and from eternity in hell. However, there is only one requirement for this great gift to us. Each and every one of us must trust in his promises and accept Jesus personally as their Savior (John 3: 16-17). God does not save mankind by groups or churches or religions but by each person individually. All other religions require man to do something to 'get right' with their God, which unfortunately only leads to them to a 'dead' end. Christianity is the only faith where God came down to man to offer free eternal life with him. This indescribable offer is open to everyone who seeks it. You have the free will to put your trust and faith and yield your life to him or not. Nothing else is needed (Acts 16: 29-31). It's that simple. Just invite him in. A new joy-filled life here on Earth and then eternity in heaven is the gift God offers. So, now comes the most important question and decision you'll ever make in your entire life. Will you place your faith in life in Christ and receive that great free gift? Now is the moment of decision. Choose wisely as your eternity hangs in the balance.

Q9 WHAT DOES IT MEAN TO WORSHIP GOD?

Worship is the grateful response to a gracious and loving God (Psalm 29: 1-2). It means honoring the God of creation who has given life and the assurance of eternal life for all who put their trust in Jesus Christ as Lord and Savior (1 Peter: 3-5). Worship is a spontaneous and voluntary act of gratitude offered by the saved sinner to the Savior. Simply stated, worship is just saying "thank you God for all your blessings" (2 Chronicles 29: 25-30). The fact is that every good thing a person has in life is a gift from God (James 1:17). So in worship, we praise God for his amazing works in creation. We praise him because his power is great and his unfailing love is even greater. In a greater sense, worship reflects the condition of the human heart and lifts the human spirit. Worship connects people with God at the spiritual level. In the Christian perspective, stewardship is worship. Service in missions and in the church is worship. Good works, done in Jesus name, is worship. Singing praises to the Lord is worship. Sharing the good news of the Gospel with others is worship. In other words, all of life's activities should be worship. Worship will be one of the primary activities for eternity in heaven (Revelation 5: 11-14). In worship, we say "to God be the glory. Great things he has done!" This is what it means to worship God.

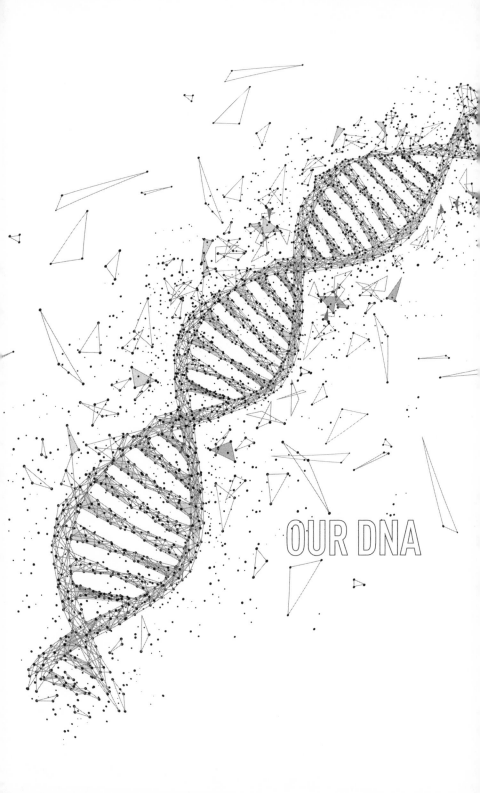

OUR DNA

CHAPTER 3

CREATION — "IN THE BEGINNING"

The most remarkable words for all humanity are found in the Bible, Genesis 1:1, "In the beginning God created the heavens and the Earth." In the beginning God spoke and the universe we know began; yes, out of nothing! Now 14 billion years later it is still being "stretched out" at just the right rate to allow life on planet Earth to survive and flourish. It is truly an amazing creation with every variable perfectly fine-tuned such that only a wise intelligent designer, God, could have possible orchestrated. This concept is referred to as the anthropic principle and is explained in this chapter. As you explore the questions that follow, you will be confronted with ideas that are both inspiring and thought-provoking and will challenge your worldview. These searching questions are those top-of-mind for our contemporary generation. They have been selected for the strong likelihood that in examining them you will gain a greater love for God, his awesome power and his marvelous creation. Enjoy your journey through the answers to the nine questions that follow.

QUESTIONS CONCERNING CREATION

Q1 HOW COULD GOD MAKE SOMETHING, CREATION, OUT OF NOTHING?

This question is in a way a mystery but there is a simple answer... because he is God and he can. As such, he is the creator of all and has existed forever. In the Bible God is referred to as I Am. But, a more explanatory answer is that he is a "transcendent" God, meaning He is in a separate world of dimensions well beyond ours and is not limited to time and space as we humans are. With God, there is no beginning and no end. He "spoke" our universe into existence through the power of his word and both time and space were created. We are unable, in our limited dimensions to comprehend this fact. We also cannot understand time. It just is! It is there to mark the days and years and the seasons of life. But, God did give us practical, positive, and understandable evidence of his existence and presence and creative power. A few examples are:

- **Nature**: the greatness, grandeur, and magnificence of all on this Earth, and the laws that govern the sciences.
- **Life**: the concept of all that is living and how it fits together for reproduction and existence. We know that humans are made in the image of God (Genesis 1:27).
- **The Bible**: We know it is God's inspired word because only He sees all of human history as if it has already happened. That's how the Bible can record hundreds of prophecies that have come to pass. That is God's omniscience and power on display.
- **Divine Intervention**: God heals diseases, answers

prayers, influences our decisions, and most importantly transforms our lives. Examples of these are endless. Think about John Newton, author of *Amazing Grace*. God transformed him from slave trader to preacher and hymn writer.

In summary, God created the universe out of nothing because he wanted to demonstrate his love for all who desire a personal relationship with him in his life and for all eternity in a new dimension, heaven. That relationship and salvation are both possible for all those who trust in Jesus as Savior and Lord.

Q2 WHAT IS MEANT BY INTELLIGENT DESIGN OF NATURE?

Intelligent design is the theory that there is a guiding force behind the creation of the universe and everything in it. The first verse of the Bible, Genesis 1:1, posits a created universe. Subsequent verses describe the work of a creator who rationally designs the solar system, the earth, and all living flora and fauna. It provides a basis for understanding science, mathematics, genetics, and man's ability to think and reason. Intelligent design presupposes a designer and therefore suggests that there is a purpose to . Since we're talking about creating something out of nothing, the "intelligence" behind the design must be a transcendent being, one that is not made of the same matter of its creation. That transcendent being or intelligent designer is called God.

Q3 IRREDUCIBLE COMPLEXITY — HOW DOES IT RELATE TO CREATION/INTELLIGENT DESIGN?

Irreducible complexity is a specific example of intelligent design. The definition of intelligent design is that the best explanation for the creation of the universe was by an intelligent cause or agent and not by natural selection (evolution). Irreducible complexity is a term that describes a system having a specific function due to several interacting parts or processes where the removal of any one of the parts or processes causes the system to cease functioning. The simplest example most often used is the mousetrap. Each of the mousetrap's parts is required for it to function as intended. The removal of any part renders the mousetrap useless as a mousetrap. Scientific advances of the last 50 years have uncovered many more processes that are irreducibly complex particularly processes in the human cell that are essential to life. Some examples:

Blood clotting is a cascade of 21 steps each leading to the next step and dependent on the step before such that the removal of any step renders the blood unable to clot. A myriad of transport systems within the cell to ferry molecules to their location for utilization.

Light sensing systems in animal eyes. The synthesis of a protein requires a multitude of steps the removal of any part would make the synthesis impossible. Biological motor systems such as that found in the bacterial flagellum. The cilia, small hairs, in our noses that move fluid over surfaces.

The reason examples of irreducible complexity are taken seriously by evolutionists is that it threatens evolution as the complete explanation of creation and the origin of man.

Charles Darwin in his *Origin of Species* stated, "If it could be demonstrated that any complex organ existed which could not possibly have been formed by numerous, successive, slight modifications, my theory would absolutely break down." Evolution is threatened because if a process will not function with the absence of any part performing its intended function how could the total process function over the time taken for the individual parts to become functional. Irreducibly complex processes seem to not have come together gradually and are examples of exquisite intelligent design.

(Text provided by G. Lee Southard, Ph.D. Author of the book, To Know With Certainty)

Q4 WHAT IS THE ANTHROPIC PRINCIPLE AS AN ARGUMENT FOR GOD?

Simply stated, it is the fine-tuning of the universe to allow life on Earth, creation. For decades scientists have been discovering properties the universe must have that make inevitable the existence of intelligent life. The more that is discovered the more amazing it is just how many properties must be precisely fine-tuned so that Earth is capable of sustaining all life forms including human beings. Today, the number of known universe characteristics recognized as fine-tuned for life is 38. Of these, the most sensitive is the space energy density (the self stretching property of the universe). Its value cannot vary by more than one part in 10 to the 120th power and still allow for the kinds of stars and planets physical life requires. This is the Cosmological Constant. In other words, the odds that any given planet in the universe would possess the necessary conditions to support intelligent physical life is one in a number so large it might as well be infinity. Here are some simple factors to remember about the Anthropic Principle:

- Expansion rate of the universe. Psalm 104:2
- Moon-Earth gravitational interaction. 'Think tides'
- Earth's precise distance from the sun. 'Cool Phase'
- Earth's magnetic force field. 'Think deflection of space debris'.
- Earth's angle of inclination and rotation rate.
- Precise composition of Earth's atmosphere.
- Lineup of the planets in our solar system.—The big gaseous planets absorb lots of space junk.
- Our Solar system's position in the Milky Way galaxy. Enables man to observe the universe.

Final thoughts. God created the universe so we could exist. We exist so we can see that only God could have created such a complex and fine-tuned universe. We exist because we are created to be Jesus' inheritance! (*"What the Father has given me."*John 10:29) As we think about the Anthropic Principle, we need to remember that the chief purpose of man is to honor God with his life and work and enjoy being in God's presence now and for eternity. This is only possible through a personal, life-transforming relationship with Jesus Christ. God created this magnificent universe for man to enjoy and its fine tuning confirms God's existence, as if there was ever any doubt!

Q5 IF MOSES WROTE GENESIS, WHERE DID HE GET ALL THE INFORMATION ON CREATION AND ON PEOPLE LIKE ADAM, NOAH, AND ABRAHAM?

First, it is important to note that Biblical scholars and theologians, both Jewish and Christian, agree that Moses wrote Genesis. Moses was educated in the pharaoh's courts in Egypt and most likely was conversant in several languages including Hebrew, the native tongue of his mother and nursemaid, Egyptian, and the Semitic language of the Midianites in whose land Moses sojourned for 40 years after fleeing Egypt when he was 40 years old.

Now for the interesting aspect of how Moses got all the details from God. When Moses led the Israelites out of Egypt, they wandered in the wilderness for 40 years because that generation did not trust God and refused to conquer the land God promised them. They complained that there were giants in the land that they could not subdue. God would have given them the victory if they had trusted, but they did not.

During those 40 years, God met with Moses frequently in the 'tent of meeting'. God gave him the true story of creation, the history of mankind and the calling of Abraham to begin a nation of God's chosen people. Those people, the Israelites, were supposed to show the world who God was and what He was all about—his love, his mercy and his power. Unfortunately, over time the Israelites, in spite of Moses' warnings, disobeyed God's commands, worshiped idols and lost God's blessings and divine providence. The Israelites were set aside as a nation, but through a series of prophets sent by God, were assured that one day in the future a savior would deliver Israel and the nation would regain the prominence it had during the reigns of kings David and Solomon. That savior, or messiah, finally arrived with the advent of Jesus who, through his death, resurrection and ascension has provided a way for Israel and all the world to be reconciled with God.

Q6 IS THERE ANY EVIDENCE TO INDICATE HOW LONG AGO GOD CREATED ADAM?

In light of all the recent discoveries, this is a great question and one in which there are a number of possibilities. Let's begin with Scripture. A literal reading of the genealogy as recorded in the book of Genesis would place Adam—a created being who possessed the ability to speak and communicate with God, and other created beings—about 6000 years ago (4000 BC). However, the Hebrew word for 'Son of' or 'Bar', later 'Ben', also means grandson of, great grandson of, etc., so there could be very many generations between each person named. Just as in later instances, only the noteworthy or significant individuals are identified.

So, the first human, one who is made in the image of God, with free will, an eternal soul and eternal life, can be identified by DNA as a homo sapien. All life created before Adam suffered death not because of sin but beacause death is the end result of life. For example, when Adam sinned by disobeying God he inherited spiritual death and that condition was passed along to all the future generations. From anthropologists we are pretty certain that there existed a people group in Asia, modern day China, with language, a city, buildings, etc. around 10,000 BC, or 12,000 years ago. Other communities in the Middle East and Africa may be older still. The best available science places the origin of humanity much farther back, at least 45,000 years. So, how old is Adam? We don't know. However, on the Reasons to

Believe website (www.reasons. org) Dr Hugh Ross and his team have done an outstanding job harmonizing the Bible and science.

Q7 IS GOD STILL ACTIVE AND INVOLVED IN HIS CREATION? PART 1

Now by its very nature this question implies that God was once active in his creation but is God still involved? If God is still involved, what is the evidence? Let's see. We need to examine our time perspective in relation to God's. The scientific interpretation of the Genesis description of creation is that the universe was created out of nothing about 13.8 billion years ago. Earth was created 4.8 billion years ago. Homo sapiens, represented by Adam, have been on Earth at least 45,000 That may seem long, but in the scheme of creation, it's a blink of an eye. So we are seeking a look at God's activity during a very, very small window. Nevertheless, we see it. The Bible records numerous instances of God being active in his creation within this small window of time.

He was involved directly with people who had personal encounters with him: Adam and Eve, Noah, Abraham, Isaac, Jacob, Moses, the Prophets, Jesus, Paul the Apostle and the disciples John and Peter just to name a few.

He was also involved with activities: the creation itself, the Flood, the Exodus out of Egypt, the occupation of the Promised Land, and the Israelites throughout the period chronicled in the Old Testament. Then there was a period of about 400 years between the Old and New Testament when God seemed to be silent. That period ended with the coming of John the Baptist to pave the way for the ministry of Jesus who equated John with Elijah (Luke 1:17). The lesson to be remembered about the silent period is that the silence of God for a period of time is not to be taken as the absence of God. Remember God is not governed by time, rather, God acted in the fullness of time, at the perfect time in history to bring Jesus to mankind. It was an act predestined by God in his plan before the creation of the world (Ephesians 1: 4-7).

Q8 IS GOD STILL ACTIVE AND INVOLVED IN HIS CREATION? PART 2

In the prior question, we covered God's involvement in his creation up to the coming of Christ. That included a silence period of 400 years before we learn of John the Baptist who announces the arrival of God's son, Jesus. God again appeared and became actively involved to complete a plan He had before the creation of the world. So let's now look at what we observe God doing after this silent period. First, we see God active as evidenced in the birth, life, death, and resurrection of Jesus, the sending of the promised Holy Spirit at Pentecost, the conversion of Paul and perhaps other unrecorded events. We may not physically see God's activity as much in Western culture today, especially Europe, but God seems to be active in other cultures. Many in these cultures throughout Africa and Asia are coming to believe in Christ in huge numbers.

God's activity is being expressed through the Holy Spirit much like it was in the first and second centuries. God's work from the beginning has always been the redemption of sinners from all nations (John 6:29). The Bible is clear on how God is involved today.

In the past God spoke to our ancestors through the prophets at many times and in various ways, but in these last days he has spoken to us by his Son, whom he appointed heir of all things, and through whom he also made the universe (Hebrews 1:1-2).

Today God speaks through the Holy Spirit that Jesus promised to send following his resurrection and through his inspired word, the Bible. However, when we ask about God's activity we should be considering our own activity. Are you sharing the "good news" of the Gospel, as you go about in your world each day? God still works through Jesus' disciples to bring hope, love and peace to a hurting world that He loves. Finally, with the coming of Jesus, God began a new way to be active with his creation. He became active through the Holy Spirit. You must connect with God on a spiritual level and in turn he acts with us on a spiritual level to bring about his plan of redemption (John 4:24) and one day Jesus will return, perhaps soon. Remember to take time away from your worldly activities to be spiritually involved with him. God is always available. He's waiting for you to call.

Q9 DO I HAVE TO CHOOSE BETWEEN MY CHRISTIAN FAITH AND WHAT SCIENCE TEACHES?

No. The Christian faith can be harmonized with the scientific facts. Science now confirms that the intricacy and complexity of the design details in both the macro (cosmic) and micro (biological) sciences point to an intelligent designer. That designer is God. Recent scientific discoveries cast great doubt on evolutionary theory. No matter how many eons of time one selects, the mathematical probability of evolution producing life forms is zero. Even though scientists now believe that the universe came into being with the Big Bang, about 13.8 billion years ago and the earth was formed about 4.8 billion years ago, in all that time, the extensive number of fossils discovered, including those in the Cambrian strata (billions upon billions of fossils), not a single transitional species was found. All fossil species appear distinct; that is no evolution. The foundation of the evolution theory is a gradual transition of species through random probabilistic transition. This is the essence of the theory yet NOT ONE transitional species has ever been found where there should be billions if not trillions. Remember this too. The older Earth's age does not conflict with the Genesis seven days of creation because the Hebrew word for day, 'ium', has four possible meanings one of which is, "A long period of time," which could be millions or billions of years. In other words, God took his time to get earth ready.

Regarding evolution, one must keep in mind that evolution was a theory which is now a worldview masquerading as scientific fact. It is fundamentally the religion of atheists who reject the idea of God or even an intelligent designer and that a human being has an eternal soul. Why? So that atheists can be their own god, live life as they please, fabricate their own truth and believe that life ends at death with no judgment day and no eternal condemnation or punishment. In other words, a life with no hope, no meaning, and no purpose of any eternal value, i.e. that human life has no value greater than that of the animals. Finally, despite overwhelming evidence, evolutionists say," my mind is made up; don't confuse me with the scientific facts or the idea of intelligent design by a creator God." So sad!! So, choose faith and study more about how science supports the Genesis account of creation. While you are searching for truth, you will also discover God's plan for your life.

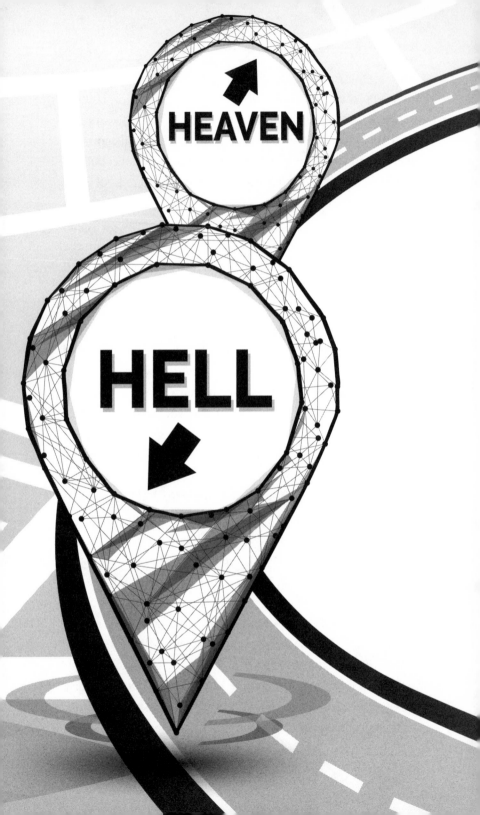

CHAPTER 4

HEAVEN AND HELL

These two subjects, **heaven** and **hell**, are perhaps a couple of the most difficult question topics to answer. The Bible has many references to these two places. Jesus talked about both of them extensively. Most people want to believe that heaven is real and that hell is not. In this chapter, we have selected 11 of the most intriguing questions that have been asked of the us over the past 5 years since we first published the original *Answers* booklet and launched our ministry website. I believe that clearly God wants every person to know that these are real places and his desire is that their choice would be heaven, not hell. The Bible clearly states that Jesus is the only way God has provided for getting access to heaven. All persons have free will to choose to accept God's ways, Jesus, or the world's way that leads to destruction. It is the most important decision anyone can ever make. We trust the excitement of being in the presence of God and Christ for eternity and the endless wonderment of heaven will be sufficient for you to make the wise choice. Now let your journey of discovery continue with the next set of questions and answers.

QUESTIONS CONCERNING HEAVEN

QUESTIONS CONCERNING HELL

Q1 **IS HEAVEN REAL OR A MYTH?**

The Bible says that heaven is a real place prepared for all who love God and have trusted in Jesus Christ as their Savior and Lord (See Revelation 21:1). Finally, Jesus said to his disciples then and for those who have trusted him down through the ages and now:

> "And if I go and prepare a place for you, I will come back and take you to be with me that you also may be where I am" (John 14:3).

The Bible says:

> "What no eye has seen, what no ear has heard, and what no human mind has conceived"—the things God has prepared for those who love him" (1 Corinthians 2:9).

Yes, heaven is for real, it's not a myth! It is God's ultimate gift to all who believe.

Q2 **ARE HEAVEN AND ETERNAL LIFE THE SAME OR DIFFERENT SOMEHOW?**

The short answer is yes and yes. In one sense, they are the same. Heaven is a place where time will not exist as we know it on Earth. This means life in heaven will be eternal; no more death. Heaven is a place Jesus promised for all who put their trust and faith in him as their Savior. He is the only way to that eternal place of peace, joy, abundant love and eternal life. In John 14:3, Jesus said "I go to prepare a place for you, so that where I am you may be also." That is one of the greatest promises ever made to mankind. It's called God's grace. God giving us something we did not deserve and never could earn by our own good works.

In another sense, eternal life is much more than heaven. Jesus said:

> "Now this is eternal life: that they know you, the only true God, and Jesus Christ, whom you have sent" (John 17:3).

What this simply means is that when you have an intimate personal life with Jesus as your Lord and Savior you have eternal life here and now. Then you will experience an abundant and exciting adventure with the one through whom God created the entire universe. As you let Jesus transform your life into his image you will see and experience life as you never could have imagined. Then you have eternal life and your spirit/soul will never die. It will go to heaven where one day you will get a glorious new eternal body. That is the good news of the gospel of Jesus Christ.

Q3 IS THERE A SECOND CHANCE PLACE SUCH AS PURGATORY? REINCARNATION?

This profound question really gets to a key truth of the Christian faith. A short quick answer is NO. The Bible says that after we die there are NO second chances. God gave us this life to make our decision and, as in Jesus' teaching in Luke 16:19-31, death is final. There are many more verses to reaffirm this. There is NOT ONE verse in scripture mentioning purgatory, which was popularized in the church in the 12th century and then became official in the 13th when Pope Innocent defined purgatory in 1254. There are verses, however, that remind us that once we have the Holy Spirit within us, he will be working to help us be conformed to Christ. But the notion that upon death we go into a holding pattern and that we get cleaned up so we can proceed to heaven has no basis in the Bible. Further, the idea that the living can do something or pay some fee to reduce the time that a dead person remains in a state of limbo while being "purged' has been rejected by Bible scholars for more than 500 years. When we die, time ends for us. At that point we are with God in heaven or without God in hell.

If that is the case, then reincarnation as taught by some eastern faiths cannot be true. When we die, we are not recycled as other people or other animals. Scripture tells us all animals and plants are specific creations of God and not previous or reincarnated humans. The Bible is very clear, when we die, if we have believed in Jesus Christ as our Savior and Lord, we will be with him in some new bodily form, recognizable, knowing others, and able to communicate with and worship him for eternity. How about you? Have you made that decision for a new joy filled life here on earth and knowing without any doubt that you will be with God forever?

Q4 WHAT WILL CHRISTIAN RESURRECTION BODIES BE LIKE?

This is a very familiar question asked by many. It's the same question that the apostle Paul answers in 1 Corinthians 15:35-52. He uses the analogy of the seed and the flower.

Our earthly bodies are like the seed. Our heavenly bodies are like the flower. The seed and the flower are very different as our earthly bodies and our heavenly bodies will be. The seed is buried in the earth and a beautiful flower emerges. Our present bodies are appropriate for this life on planet Earth but God is going to give us new, glorious spiritual bodies suited for the life to come.

We do not know all the details of our resurrection bodies because quite frankly they are beyond our human understanding. As Paul wrote,

"Listen, I tell you a mystery . . . we will all be changed—in a flash, in the twinkling of an eye" 1 Corinthians 15:51-52.

that said, however, we do know that we will recognize each other in our new glorious bodies. Those bodies will be without sin, sickness, sorrow, weakness, and we will never die.

Our resurrection bodies will be eternal and nothing can ever again separate us from the love of Christ, our Lord. We will be united with those believers and family members we have loved and been apart from for awhile. This is all we really need to know about what our resurrection heavenly bodies will be like. The rest we can leave to God. Jesus said, "And if I go and prepare a place for you, I will come back and take you to be with me that you also may be where I am" John 14:3.

Jesus will be coming only for those for whom he is savior and lord. Jesus is coming again (1 Thessalonians 4:16). Are you ready for his return?

Q5 WHAT IS THE THIRD HEAVEN?

Three thousand years ago science did not have the benefit of the Hubble telescope or a way to express mankind's observation of the earth's atmospheric makeup. In Isaiah 55: 9-10 the description of heaven refers to what we know now as our atmosphere and the air we breathe. It was identified as the "first heaven", which can now be observed from the international manned space station. In the book of Genesis 1:4-17, Moses is describing the cosmos or universe that contains the stars and galaxies and the black holes and much more. This created universe is what would be called the "second heaven". Romans 1:9-10 tells us that this universe discloses the glory of its creator, God, so that man is without excuse for not recognizing him as the intelligent designer of our magnificent universe. The "third heaven" is the destination of those who placed their faith and trust in Jesus Christ as Savior and Lord. It exists in a dimension outside of our universe. It is referred to in 2 Corinthians 12:2, where a man "was caught up to the third heaven." Today it is known as just Heaven, the dwelling place of God, of Jesus Christ, the angels and those who have physically died and are now spiritually alive. This latter group includes those who died prior to Jesus' time who trusted by faith in God such as Abraham, Joseph, Moses, Daniel and the prophets. Glimpses into the third heaven were experienced by several individuals including Stephen, a follower of Christ, (Acts 7:55-56), Ezekiel, an Old Testament prophet (Ezekiel 1:24-28), Daniel, a Hebrew captive who served in the court of a Babylonian ruler (Daniel 7:9-14), and John, one of Jesus' dearest friends and apostle (Revelation 21). What God has planned for those that love him, trust him and know Jesus as Savior is beyond anything one could ever dream or imagine.

Q6 WHAT DOES HEAVEN LOOK LIKE?

Wouldn't we all like to know exactly what God has created in Heaven. The Bible says this about Heaven,

> "'What no eye has seen, what no ear has heard, and what no human mind has conceived' the things God has prepared for those who love him" (1 Corinthians 2:9).

In other words, heaven is magnificent, wonderful, awesome, beautiful and beyond human description. Picture the most beautiful exotic place on earth only infinitely better. And yes, while heaven is a mystery it piques our curiosity and our desire to know more. The Scriptures have provided some glimpses into heaven for us to anticipate as God has revealed them to us by his Spirit. That means God has given us some 'sneak previews' to whet our desire to go there one day. To have the fun of discovering for yourself, look up the following scripture references; Ezekiel 1:24-28, Daniel 7:9-14, and Revelation 21. You will be awestruck at the descriptions in these visions God provided. Heaven will be a place of endless wonderment in the presence of God and Jesus and the saints of all the ages! Remember, heaven is only for those that have placed their faith and trust in Jesus Christ as Savior and Lord (John 14:6).

Q7 HOW DO WE GET TO HEAVEN?

Wouldn't that be nice to know for certain. Well, we can. As Jesus said in John 14:6, "I am the way, the truth and the life; no one comes to the Father except through me." Since God the Father resides in another dimension that is called heaven, Jesus is the only way to get there. When Jesus came to earth, "Emmanuel, God with us," he came from heaven and certainly knew the way back. The good news is that he has gone there to prepare a place for all those who have a personal faith relationship with him. But the question remains, how do we actually find heaven knowing Jesus is the way. Well now, there is some evidence from people's personal end-of-life experiences that suggest that God sends a guardian angel to guide the saved person's eternal soul to heaven the moment their physical body dies. That reality should give us some comfort. We do know for certain that the angels are God's messengers to take on whatever task they are assigned. Some of those tasks involved visits to earth such as Gabriel telling Mary and Joseph about the coming virgin birth of their son who would be the messiah, the savior promised to the Hebrews, God's chosen people (Luke 1:26-38). An angel also came to a priest named Zechariah to tell him that his wife, Elizabeth, Mary's cousin, would conceive even in her old age and give birth to a son, John the Baptist (Luke 1:5-25). Then there were the two angels that warned Lot and his family to leave Sodom and Gomorrah (Genesis 19:1-3). So, if the angels knew how to get to earth from heaven, they certainly know the way to return. Wouldn't it be nice to have an angel as your guide.

Q8 IS HELL A REAL PLACE?

The simple answer is yes. The Bible makes more references, over 65, to hell than to heaven. It is described as a place of eternal torment, utter darkness, constant weeping, no water to quench one's thirst and a place of eternal fire. There are personal true testimonies of people who had out of body experiences and were headed through a dark tunnel to hell. The pain they reported to have experienced was unbearable. In "Inferno," the first section of *Divine Comedy*, the 14th century epic poem written by Dante Alighieri, the poet describes an unspeakably gruesome picture of what hell might be like. The reality is most assuredly much worse...and there is no escape. Why is the Bible so graphic about hell? Because God does not want anyone to go there. God gives all mankind frequent and significant warnings about the destiny of those who reject God's offer of salvation in Jesus Christ. The choice is clear heaven or hell both are real places.

Q9 IS EVIL AN ILLUSION OR REALITY?

Some religions suggest that evil is just an illusion. That it is a condition of the mortal mind. Others have said it is a result of ignorance and superstitions and if you don't think about it evil will go away. Our life experiences argue otherwise. We lock our cars and houses. We have security systems. We have laws against murder, rape, lying under oath, etc. Yes evil is real. It reared its ugly head in the garden of evil when Adam and Eve used their gift of free will to disobey God (Genesis 3). There was only one commandment and they chose not to keep it. At that moment, the human race and the earth began to experience the opposite of God's goodness, evil. Evil is the absence of God. We see it expressed in pain, suffering, discord, war and death. The 'good news' is that God reigns and one day evil will be overthrown. All those who put their trust in him will live eternally where there is no pain, no suffering and no death.

Q10 WHY DID JESUS TALK MORE ABOUT HELL THAN HEAVEN?

Jesus spoke more of hell than Heaven but we do know He spoke a lot about both. You know God tells us that He loved us so much that

" . . . while we were still sinners Christ died for us" (Romans 5:8).

So God's purpose for each of us has to bring us into a present and future heavenly relationship with them. So warning us of the consequences of not getting our hearts and lives to Christ is a further evidence of this love for us. Jesus it seems wanted to make the choice simple and obvious. It is similar to you and your children whom you love. If you see them entering a dangerous situation don't you immediately warn and stop them and tell them of the danger? Christ's persistent warnings about hell tells us that it is a real place and He doesn't want anyone to go there. Remember, a person's ultimate destination at death is either Heaven or hell. The point is that Jesus is saying that there is existence beyond physical death and there are only two possible outcomes. The fact is that God would have come to know and trust him and gain eternal life, but He gave everyone the free will to choose. So, how about you? Have you come into that life-transforming personal relationship with Jesus and know for sure where you will be for eternity? "If you declare with your mouth, 'Jesus is Lord', and believe in your heart that God raised him from the dead, you will be saved.

> "For it is with your heart that you believe and are justified, and it is with your mouth that you profess your faith and are saved" (Romans 10:9-10).

Q11 WILL THE 'LOST OR UNSAVED' HAVE BODIES IN HELL OR ONLY TORMENTED SOULS?

This somewhat perplexing question has been considered many times, down through the ages, by Christians and non-Christians alike. Seven hundred years ago. Dante Alighieri wrote his epic poem, *Divine Comedy*, in which he imagines what torment might be like in various levels of hell. The first section of the poem, entitled "Inferno," is one of literature's most disturbing perspectives on torment in hell for body and soul. While Dante's imaginings are instructive, we always look to see what God has said in his inspired word, the Bible.

In many Biblical references hell is described as a real place, a place that was initially created for Satan and the fallen angels (Jude 1:6). It is also a place for all those who have rejected God's free gift of redemption and salvation in his son, Jesus Christ. The scriptures are very clear that there is no condemnation or punishment or torment for those who have trusted in Jesus as Savior and Lord (Romans 8:1). That's the good news!

Jesus, who spoke more about hell than heaven, described hell as a place where there will be weeping and gnashing of teeth. Note that Jesus is describing a place populated by physical beings, not ethereal spirits. The pain and anguish will be very real. In the book of Revelation, John refers to the resurrection of the dead non-believers with bodies. Paul, in his letter to the church at Philippi writes:

"every knee should bow, in heaven and on earth and under the earth, and every tongue acknowledge that Jesus Christ is Lord, to the glory of God the Father" (Philippians 2:10,11).

Unfortunately, it will be too late for those who die without choosing to follow Jesus. In Hebrews 9:27 we read that man dies once and then faces judgement. In the book of Revelation, John writes that the unsaved will stand before God in judgment and be cast into hell or the lake of fire for all eternity (Revelation 20:11-15). Finally, the unsaved will be in constant torment and anguish. They will forever regret their choice to reject Jesus. They will lament over thoughts like, "if I had only listened," or "if I hadn't been so stubborn," or "if I had only believed," or "if I only trusted in Jesus." God gives everyone an equal chance to have eternal life and be forever with him in heaven. So choose wisely while there is yet time. Jesus is calling. We trust that you will say yes.

COME,
FOLLOW
ME.

CHAPTER 5

JESUS — EMMANUEL — GOD WITH US

Jesus, God's only son, born in a stable in Bethlehem, lived a perfect sinless life, taught truth with authority and performed countless miracles including raising the dead. He took the penalty for man's sin by giving up his life on a cross. After three days he came back to life whereupon he was seen by his disciples and over 500 others. Then he returned to heaven, his original home, and resumed his position at the right hand of God.

Over the centuries since Jesus' ascension to heaven, there have been many questions about who he really was or is: a prophet? a teacher? an itinerant rabbi? God in human form? Or was he, as 20th Century theologian C.S. Lewis pondered, "a lunatic or something worse."

Each person must make his or her own decision about what to do with Jesus. And trying to decide, the sincere curious seeker has many genuine questions. We have tackled just a few of those which are answered in the pages that follow. We trust you will find them of value and cause you to know Jesus on a personal basis as your Savior.

QUESTIONS CONCERNING JESUS

Q1 IS JESUS REALLY GOD?

Yes. It is the foundational belief of Christianity. It is a belief based on the actions, teachings and writings of Jesus and the men and women who knew him. They are recorded in the Bible, a book that is recognized universally as the best preserved collection of literature from the ancient world. Prominent in the ministry of Jesus was the miracles he performed. Here are just a few:

- Jesus heals the sick (Matthew 8:1-14).
- Jesus calms the storm, demonstrating his power over nature. There were 12 witnesses (Matthew 8:26).
- Jesus walks on water in front of 12 witnesses (Matthew 14:25,26, John 6:19).
- Jesus raises Lazarus from the dead (John 11:42). This was done in front of many witnesses including those who reported what they saw to the leaders of the Jewish community. Only God has the power to raise the dead.
- Jesus gives sight to the blind (John 9:1-12).
- Jesus is transfigured and becomes radiant in glory upon a mountain (Matthew 17:1-8, Mark 9:2-8, Luke 9:28-36). James, Peter and John were witnesses.
- Jesus comes back from the dead (Matthew 28:6 and Mark 16:6). He walked the Earth for 40 days after he had risen. He was seen by the 11 disciples plus the women who visited the tomb and more than 500 others (Matthew 27:52).
- Jesus ascended into heaven (Mark 16:19, Luke 24:50 and Acts 1:19). There were at least 11 witnesses.

In addition to these well-documented events, John, the disciple who may have been closest to Jesus, affirms his divinity (John 1:1, and 1:14 and John 21:25).

The Apostle Paul writes in the letter to the church at Philippi,

> "at the name of Jesus every knee will bow and every tongue confess that Jesus Christ is Lord" (Philippians 2:10-11).

In the eighth chapter of John, Jesus answers his critics by explaining, in a variety of ways, that he is God. Towards the end of the discussion, he challenged their understanding of the first patriarch of the Jewish people and when challenged about his age he said:

> "Before Abraham was born, I am!" (John 8:58).

With that statement, the religious leaders of the day knew exactly what Jesus was saying, because only the one true God referred to himself as "I am." Here Jesus affirms that he is God. He is the eternal one. In John 14:9-10, Jesus further explains:

> "Anyone who has seen me has seen the Father."

The only logical conclusion from these statements is that Jesus is who He claims to be. He is Emmanuel, God with us. He is the great "I am." He is the creator of the universe and all life.

Q2 DID JESUS CLAIM TO BE GOD?

YES. There are so very many instances where Jesus said he was God. (See the preceding answer.) He stated clearly, ". . . anyone who has seen me has seen the Father . . ." (John 14:9). ". . . I and the Father are one . . ." (John 10:30). He repeatedly referred to himself as "I am" (John 8:58) which in the Hebrew tradition amounted to a declaration that he was God. It was these repeated pronouncements that infuriated the Pharisees (Jewish religious leaders in Jesus' time) and ultimately caused them to demand his execution. On one occasion, Jesus invited three of his disciples, James, Peter and John, to accompany him to Mt. Tabor to witness him being transfigured to the majesty and glory he had before coming to Earth. There Jesus was joined in midair by Moses and Elijah and the witnesses heard the voice of God saying,

"This is my Son, whom I love; with him I am well pleased. Listen to him!" (Matthew 17:5).

Furthermore, Jesus raised several people from the dead including Lazarus, a man who had been dead four days and was starting to stink of decay (John 11: 17&39). There were many witnesses to these events.

Most significantly, Jesus, himself, rose from the dead, one of the most documented events of the ancient world. Following his resurrection, Jesus appeared in bodily form to hundreds of people and during this period he would suddenly appear and disappear through doors and walls in a locked room. The evidences are many and clear. His coming to Earth, living a perfect life, performing many miracles, suffering a terrible death for us on a cross and rising from the dead that we may be forgiven and enjoy fellowship with him now here on this earth is sufficient to confirm that Jesus is indeed God. All it takes is for you to say yes, I believe and trust in him. Have you? If not, why not?

Q3 WAS JESUS THE PROMISED MESSIAH?

According to the Bible, Jesus is the anointed one, or Messiah, who would become king at the end of days. In the New Testament portion of the Bible, the life and work of Jesus reveals that he fulfills more than 300 specific prophecies that were recorded hundreds of years before his birth. The fulfilled prophecies point to more than just an anointed king, but also a suffering savior, a teacher, and a healer. More than 400 years passed between the time when God spoke to his chosen people, the Hebrews in the Old Testament and when he spoke again, through John the Baptist and Jesus in the New Testament. During that long time of absence, the words of the prophecy of the coming Messiah encouraged people to continue to pray and expect a king to rule them. In Jeremiah 33 we read of Jesus reestablishing God's chosen people. Micah 5:2 prophecies the birth of Jesus. But it is not until we read in John 1:19-34, the testimony of John the Baptist and his introduction of the Jesus "the Lamb of God" that we begin to see the fulfillment of the many prophecies and our understanding that Jesus is the promised Messiah.

Q4 WHAT ARE SOME OF THE PROPHECIES ABOUT JESUS AS THE MESSIAH?

First, we must recognize that the Bible is the only prophetic book that is 100% accurate and reliable. Why? Because it is God's inspired word and God knows the future because he exists outside of time and space. In fact, God sees all of time from beginning to end as if it is already an accomplished fact, which in God's view it is. Now, there are more than 300 prophecies in the Bible regarding Jesus first and second comings. First, he came as a humble servant and Savior, the Messiah. Second, he will come as the King of Kings at the end of the Tribulation period described in the books of Daniel, Ezekiel and Revelation. The odds of any one person for fulfilling even eight or 10 such prophecies is near zero. Since Jesus fulfilled hundreds, that should be sufficient to convince even a skeptic that he was and is the foretold Messiah. Unfortunately, many have made up their minds to reject Jesus as the Messiah in spite of the overwhelming evidence. They choose to do so of course at their own eternal peril. So in answer to your question, here are a few prophetic references that predate Jesus by more than 400 years. As you review them, you can decide if Jesus is the Messiah.

1. **Genesis 3:15 & Isaiah 7:14** — Seed of a woman (virgin birth)
2. **Micah 5:2** — Born in Bethlehem Ephrathah (also city of King David's birth)
3. **Isaiah 53:1** — Rejection by ruling Jews of Jesus' day
4. **Psalm 22:14 -17** — Jesus to die by crucifixion (not a method of killing until the Romans introduced it 1000 years later)

5. **Exodus 12:46** — His bones not to be broken (It was common practice for the Romans to break the bones of the person being crucified to hasten death, Jesus' weren't)
6. **Isaiah 53:5-12** — The Messiah to die as a sacrifice for sin (the Cross)
7. **Psalm 16:10** — Messiah to be resurrected (Jesus was the first to be resurrected confirming that He had conquered both sin and death

Q5 WAS JESUS' RESURRECTION REAL? IS HE STILL ALIVE TODAY?

Yes and yes. There were over 500 witnesses to Jesus' return to life after being crucified dead and buried. The Romans made no mistakes when they killed someone. They were expert at the art of death. Yet, three days later, Jesus appeared to his disciples, to several women, to two men walking on the road to Emmaus, to a doubting Thomas and two others. Jesus was definitely dead and he was definitely resurrected. His disciples witnessed his ascension into heaven (Matthew 28, Mark 16, Luke 24, John 20,21 and Acts 1). So yes, Jesus is definitely alive. It is his power and authority that holds every atom in the universe together. One day Jesus will return to Earth just like he left it to rule and reign as King of Kings. Given the events of these times it could be soon. Are you ready?

Q6 WAS JESUS' ASCENSION INTO HEAVEN WITNESSED? IF SO, BY WHOM?

A group of Jewish men, his disciples, witnesses the ascension of Jesus into heaven. This occurred after the risen Jesus appeared to both followers of Jesus and to some who were not followers. Jesus appeared first to Mary Magdalene (John 20:10-18), and then witnessed by disciples, then over 500 people. This event was monumental because prior to his ascension, He was seen for forty days as a physical human being after conquering death. Since the ascension was an integral part of the promises that Jesus made to his disciples, they rejoiced because they knew that he would be sending a Comforter (referred to as the Holy Spirit) to guide and comfort them (Matthew 28, Mark 16, Luke 24, John 20,21 and Acts 1,2).

Q7 IS JESUS REALLY COMING AGAIN?

The Bible tells us that Jesus is coming again on two occasions. The reason Jesus is coming again on the first occasion is to "take up from the earth" those who believe in him, both the living and the dead, to be with him forever. Only true believers will see Jesus at this event. This is the hope of every Christian. The rest of the world will still wonder what happened to all these people. Two of the Bible verses that describe this are:

> "For the Lord himself will come down from heaven, with a loud command, with the voice of the archangel and with the trumpet call of God, and the dead in Christ will rise first. After that, we who are still alive and are

left will be caught up together with them in the clouds to meet the Lord in the air. And so be with the Lord forever" (1 Thessalonians 4:16-17). (Note: Jesus does not set his foot on the Earth in this event.)

"I tell you, on that night two people will be in one bed; one will be taken and the other left. Two women will be grinding grain together; one will be taken and the other left" (Luke 17:34-35).

Though Biblical scholars have debated the specific timing, we believe the first event will occur either shortly before or during a time referred to as the Great Tribulation. The timing is a mystery as only God knows the day and hour for it to happen. The Tribulation is a future period of seven years of suffering and persecution, especially for the Jews, during which God will pour out his wrath on all the other unbelieving nations of the world. (See Matthew 24 for the signs of the times for the Tribulation to commence.)

The reason Jesus is coming again for the last time, which is called the Second Coming of Christ, is to fulfill his promises to defeat Satan and his army in the battle of Armageddon, and to rule the earth for a thousand years, a period referred to as the Millennial Reign. Here Jesus comes to the earth and stays for a thousand years. In Acts, we read:

They were looking intently up into the sky as he was going, when suddenly two men dressed in white stood beside them. "Men of Galilee," they said, "Why do you stand here looking into the sky? This same Jesus, who has been taken from you into heaven, will come back

in the same way you have seen him go into heaven"
(Acts 1:10-11).

This second and final return of Jesus will occur at the end
of the Tribulation. Are you reconciled with God through faith in
Jesus Christ so you will not be "left behind" to experience God's
wrath and condemnation? You must be ready today because
Jesus will come at an hour when you do not expect him.

Q8 CAN WE TRUST THAT JESUS LOVES US?

We are all broken people and we live in a broken world where
we hurt and we hurt others. Given our propensity to hurt, and
be hurt by others, it can be hard to trust anyone, especially in
God and his love for us. It is easy to look at the way others treat
us and the motives behind their actions and project that onto
God, but he never changes his mind or his word and, unlike all
of us, he is completely faithful. God loves us so much that he
sent his only son, Jesus, to die for our sin and brokenness; to
heal us and so that we could have a relationship with him, the
source of life and everything good (John 3:16). We might think
that God doesn't love us, or even that God didn't really love
his son, Jesus. After all, you may reason, he abandoned Jesus to
die a cruel and gruesome death on a cross. But, we now know
that Jesus' death was the only way for us to be made clean and
to put us in right relationship with God. God didn't abandon
Jesus. Rather, Jesus loves us so much, he voluntarily gave his
life that we may live. Sometimes, we might think that God
doesn't answer prayer and isn't there, but God will never leave
or forsake us (Deuteronomy 31:6). He answers all prayers that

align with our good, because He knows our needs better than we do (Matthew 6:8). The prayers that are guaranteed to be answered are when we pray for God's will to be done (Matthew 6:9-11). God's plans for us are far bigger than we could ever ask or imagine (Ephesians 3:20), and his plans for us are for good and not for evil (Jeremiah 29:11). God is the only one who will never fail us, and we can trust him.

Q9 WHY WOULD ANYONE WANT TO FOLLOW JESUS?

Life is about choices. Decisions we make have outcomes that impact our lives, influence our behavior, form our beliefs and define our relationships with others. We can choose to continue with business as usual, enjoying success based on the standards defined by our secular culture. Or, we can take an honest look at Jesus of the Bible and dare to ask what the consequences might be if we really believed, trusted, and obeyed him. Would following Jesus really bring life meaning, purpose, joy, peace and eternal life? For nearly 2,000 years, people around the world from every nation have been choosing to follow Jesus. They have recognized that Jesus gave his life for them and was raised from the dead so that all who follow him can enjoy God's kingdom, peace with God and everlasting life. Jesus proved that he was God by signs, miracles, profound wisdom, and overcoming death and the grave. Jesus confirmed that He is the only way to heaven and eternal life (John 14:6). So the question really is, "why wouldn't everyone want to follow Jesus?" Life is a gift from God. It can only be lived to the fullest in a relationship with Jesus. Remember happiness depends on happenings, which are temporary, but real joy and fulfillment, which are eternal, are only found in Jesus. That is why untold millions have chosen to follow him.

Q10 WHAT DOES IT MEAN TO HAVE A TRANSFORMATIONAL ENCOUNTER WITH THE PERSON OF JESUS CHRIST?

Transformation means to make a thorough or dramatic change in form, outward appearance and inward or spiritual character of a person. So, looking at it from God's perspective, the first step in the process is to personally commit your life to Jesus Christ to begin a dramatic spiritual transformation. You will come to know that he and his presence are real, both in the world and within you. It becomes the work of the Holy Spirit to guide the transformation. The principle is that God never leaves you as you were before you accepted Christ and decided to follow him. God has a much better plan for your future than you could have ever dreamed or imagined. Your life's purpose, activities, priorities, goals, worldview and much more will now be different.

The theological term is sanctification, becoming more like Jesus. Here are some of the changes you can expect. You will find yourself with a growing desire to get into God's word, the Bible, and learn and understand more about him and the Christian life. You will really hunger after his word, your "daily bread". You will begin praying more. Your prayer time will be both intimate and personal with the Lord. You will come to cherish your time together. Your friends will likely change. First, you will tell them about your new relationship and if they are not interested you will find new friendships with other believers. Conversations will change from the usual mundane topics of weather, politics, events, etc. to those of a personal spiritual nature. You will look for new frontiers in your discussions and discover how you can leave a legacy. Interest in materialism will wane and your desire for secular culture will diminish. Yes, you will continue to work and earn a living but it will no longer become the center of your life's goal. Your interests and concerns will gradually be directed towards people, not things. Emotions like hatred, jealousy, envy, etc. will, over time, become a thing of the past and be replaced with genuine caring, compassion, forgiveness and love.

You will develop a strong desire to share your faith with others because of the joy for your newly transformed life and hope within you. In this life each person thinks that he or she has the power and control over what life will be like. That discretion is called free will. When the choice is made to trust in Jesus, one becomes a "new creation in Christ" and the transformation begins. No longer does the world's value system determine life's choices, rather the Holy Spirit directs your total existence if you are willing and listen. Picture the lowly caterpillar transformed into a beautiful butterfly. That's what God's intent is for every person. That is why he sent his son Jesus Christ into the world to give each person the opportunity to know him, to live with meaning and purpose and gain eternal life. That is Transformational Encounter!

Faith
Love
Grace
Hope
HOPE
LOVE Mercy LOV
Faith
Faith Hope
Grace

CHAPTER 6

GRACE, MERCY, FAITH, HOPE, AND LOVE

Two of the most amazing gifts of God are his **love** and **grace** given to undeserving sinners. God's **love** is best expressed in the gift of his son, Jesus, and the grace that comes with him to every person of every nation who would put their faith in Jesus as Savior and Lord. God's love is offered unconditionally as He would desire that each person would come into a personal life-changing relationship with Jesus and gain eternal life. God is not only loving and the source of love but merciful, granting mercy rather than punishment and condemnation to all who trust in him. **Mercy** is not giving a person what they deserve based on their deeds. We often seek justice for wrongs we have experienced but we are much better off to receive God's mercy.

Now **faith** is defined in the Bible as being confident in what we hope for and assurance of what we do not see (Hebrews 11:1). Biblical faith is not blind faith, as some say, but faith based on the character, actions and promises of God and the evidence of God's involvement in creation, in Christ, in the inspired word and in the transformed lives of Christian believers. Finally, we have **hope**. It is a word commonly used today but with many subtle nuances. People hope things will get better, that they will be happy, successful, wealthy, famous and even be good enough to get into heaven. Unfortunately, hope is not a method or a way. Real hope is found only in Jesus as you will discover in the questions and answers on the pages that follow in this chapter.

QUESTIONS — GRACE, MERCY, FAITH, HOPE AND LOVE

Q1 WHAT IS GOD'S AMAZING GRACE?

Grace is more than the song, Amazing Grace. Yet the words of that song resound with the truth. What is amazing about God's grace is that it is a free gift. It is God reaching out to us. Yes, reaching out while we were yet sinners, Christ died for us (Romans 5:8). This is a gift offered to all who accept Jesus as Savior and Lord. God's grace is his unmerited favor bestowed upon repentant sinners. People can do nothing to earn it nor do they deserve it. It is an expression of God's love for the world he created (John 3:16). God has made loving him a simple act. As the first verse of the song says,

> "Amazing Grace how sweet the sound that saved a wretch like me.
>
> I once was lost but now am found was blind but now I see."

Those who reject God's grace and mercy will experience his judgment and his justice. We each have free will, so the choice is up to each of us: accept or reject. Choose wisely.

Q2 WHAT IS MEANT BY THE RICHES OF GOD'S GRACE?

The Bible mentions the word grace many times. The word grace is often referred to as God's unmerited favor. It is however much more than that. The word riches suggest that God's grace is extremely valuable and highly to be prized. The dimensions of God's grace are boundless and include but are not limited to his kindness, forbearance, patience, clemency, forgiveness and kindheartedness. We need to keep in mind that the Grace of God is nothing less than the unlimited love of God expressed in the gift of his son, Jesus Christ. The richness of this grace is intended to lead a person to repentance and salvation. The message in the Bible about grace is quite clear. It is that God has given mankind his richest possession, his Son Jesus, so that those who put their trust in him can have eternal life. So, we can say that in addition to being a blessing for believers, the 'Riches of God's Grace' is the offer to sinners of an unfathomable kindness, the way that God provided a pathway to reconciliation with him. The whole of heaven glorifies God for what he has done in saving sinners through Christ's death on the cross and his resurrection. There is no greater expression of love than this, God's Grace. We trust you have received this priceless gift of grace.

Q3 WHY IS THERE SUCH AN INCREDIBLE RESISTANCE TO GOD'S GRACE?

Some Bible scholars think today's resistance to the Gospel is due to the hardness of men's hearts, just as it has been since Jesus walked on this earth (Matthew 13). A greater obstacle may be procrastination. People don't think about their relationship to God until faced with great tragedy, illness and impending death. Idol worship continues to be a major stumbling block throughout the world. Materialism has replaced spirituality, which has led people to resist the loving grace of God. One of the reasons for this phenomenon is the need for instant and tangible gratification and pleasure. For example, society is bombarded with powerful substitutes through media such as movies, advertisements, social media, etc. Another reason is the growing need to compete for bigger and better everything which feeds the need to purchase unnecessary items and which drives financial decisions. Lastly, society has created a cult of celebrity whereby our adoration that should be reserved for God, is lavished on entertainers, sports stars and even politicians (Exodus 20:4). Sadly worshiping these idols brings brief satisfaction and distracts people from seeking and knowing the loving grace of God.

Q4 WHAT IS GOD'S MERCY TOWARDS SINNERS?

The Merriam-Webster dictionary defines mercy as, "compassion or forbearance shown especially to an offender." Those who disobey or break God's laws and commandments are offenders or sinners. Mercy, as used in the Scriptures, is the discretionary power of God to be compassionate. It is an act of great kindness. God showed mankind mercy combined with love when he sent his Son, Jesus, to bear man's sins in his body on the cross. God knew when he gave man free will that man would choose to use it frequently in unwise ways. History has confirmed that man has continued to make many bad choices as evidenced by the mayhem, chaos and evil that continues even in our world today. As Chuck Colson, a former convict and founder of Prison Fellowship, often said, "never underestimate the depravity of fallen sinful man." But God did something amazing because of his great love for sinners. His mercy or merciful plan was to provide a way for restoring an intimate relationship between man and himself. That plan was fulfilled in Jesus's death and resurrection. At the cross, God demonstrated two of his many attributes, mercy and love. Hearing and heeding God's words of mercy leads to faith and salvation in Christ.

Q5 WHAT DOES IT MEAN TO HAVE FAITH?

The word faith is used frequently in everyday conversations; "have faith" or "keep the faith", etc. So, what does it mean to have faith? It could mean faith that the elevator, or airplane or parachute will function as expected. It could also refer to faith or trust in the person such as a parent, teacher, coach, a friend, or a pastor. In other words someone who is reliable and trustworthy. In America people have faith that the government will protect our freedoms, provide for national security and administer justice. In these examples and others like them there are frequently disappointments. Things, people and organizations fail to always "keep the faith".

Christian faith is an entirely different matter. Faith for a Christian means absolutely trusting in God, in his sovereignty, wisdom and love. It means trusting in all God's promises, the greatest of which is that when you accept Jesus Christ as Lord and Savior you receive forgiveness of all your sins. The Spirit of God lives in you, and you receive the promise that when you die (and all do) you will enjoy the glories of heaven in the presence of the eternal God forever. Christian faith therefore is the assurance of things hoped for and the certainty of things not seen.

Why is this true? It is true because God is the one who provides that assurance and that certainty because God is faithful to do what he has promised. While no one has seen God, the evidence of God is readily available to anyone seeking to know him. The creation with all of its beauty and details and intricacy reflects its designer. The Bible, God's living word, reveals the very nature and character of God and contains all of his promises for those who put their faith in him. And finally, God revealed himself in his son Jesus Christ. It doesn't get any better than that. So, be sure your faith is in God. He never disappoints and he will always be with you.

Q6 WHAT DOES IT MEAN TO RECEIVE THE KINGDOM OF GOD LIKE A 'LITTLE CHILD'?

Jesus said, "Let the children come to me, and do not hinder them, for the kingdom of heaven belongs to such as these" (Matthew 19:14).

Jesus' statement is recorded in the three synoptic gospels (Matthew, Mark and Luke) so it is important. His disciples were annoyed about the children that were being brought to Jesus, as well as those that were pressing in to see him. Jesus saw these situations as teaching moments. A child is totally dependent on his caretaker. Think of a child. Simple, innocent, with no agenda; skipping along, going where their parent goes, trusting and asking no questions. If they let go of his or her hand and run ahead and get hurt, the parent says, "it's okay" and gently binds their wounds. "Next time you will trust me more when I caution you." When the child is troubled, the parent comforts him; and when in danger, protects him. The parent shows unconditional love for the child.

Now think of us. Are we like the child, harmless and inoffensive, free from restraint, meek, humble and without pride or personal ambitions? Or are we self-sufficient and trusting in ourselves as we navigate through life? Jesus says we must be like that innocent, trusting child, dependent on our heavenly Father to guide us through life: to such belong the kingdom of heaven. When we come as a child, our sufficiency is in Christ, not in ourselves. Have you come to Jesus with that little-child-like faith? He is waiting to receive you with open arms. Remember, Jesus is the only way to heaven and eternal life.

Q7 WHAT IS BIBLICAL LIVING HOPE? HOPE IN WHOM OR WHAT?

The word hope is commonly used to denote a deep desire, as in "I hope I get that promotion" or "I hope he proposes" or things of that sort in the temporal realm here on earth. The word hope for the Christian has a very different meaning. A Christians' hope is in the Lord. It means the absolute assurance that God's word is true and can be fully trusted now and for eternity. God has given Christians absolute hope for heaven and eternal life through the resurrection of Jesus Christ from the dead. A Christians' hope is in God's unfailing love. It enables our souls to rest in God because Biblical hope comes from him (1 Peter 1:3). Faith and hope go hand-in-hand as faith is confidence in what we hope for and assurance about what we do not yet see (Hebrews 11:1).

Hope in Christ gives believers boldness to both defend and contend for the Christian faith. The world puts out many ideas about what happens after death, but a Christian has the hope of heaven. This hope is the absolute, unwavering certainty of eternal life through Jesus Christ in a realm where there is no sickness, sin or death. That's really good news. One who has this hope can face uncertain times and even death unafraid, for the knowledge of "living, though he die" is at the bedrock of his or her hope. God has promised Christians a place that is even more perfect than any of us can ever dream or imagine and one that fulfills our greatest hopes and deepest longings (1 Corinthians 2:9). When we surrender our lives to Jesus Christ, his Holy Spirit in us quickens our spirit to have this wonderful assurance. Have you surrendered to him? There is no better time than now.

Q8 WHAT DOES GOD'S LOVE REALLY MEAN?

Agape is the Greek word used in the Bible when referring to God's love. Agape is one of the four Greek words that are often translated as love. It describes selfless love of one person for another, without any romantic implications, especially love that is spiritual in nature. Some writers have described agape as the noblest word for love in the Greek language. It is love that is given to every person from God without any preconditions. Some will choose to embrace it and others will reject it at their own peril. It is unconditional, unselfish and unbounded. It is a consuming passion for the well-being of others, a love that reflects compassion and sacrifice and is embodied in Jesus, the Christ. John, one of Jesus' dearest disciples and a writer of several of the books of the Bible, explains it this way:

> "This is love: not that we loved God, but that he loved us and sent his Son as an atoning sacrifice for our sins" (1 John 4:10).

Q9 IN WHAT WAY CAN A CHRISTIAN SHOW GOD'S LOVE?

Love is shown by putting others first . . . listening, sharing time, comforting, encouraging, smiling and doing as Jesus would do. It is shown by doing the little things daily that reflect that love . . . caring, supporting, listening, giving, sacrificing, respecting, etc. Love is shown by telling the person you love them and by doing random acts of kindness without expecting a thank you in return. Another is by honoring your father and mother, your elders, your teachers and those in authority. Love is shown by sharing the gospel message.

> "God so loved the world that he gave his one and only Son that whoever believes in him shall not perish but have eternal life" (John 3:16).

Q10 WHY DO PEOPLE STRUGGLE TO LOVE OTHERS? ISN'T THAT THE GREAT COMMANDMENT?

You can't share what you don't know personally. Some people are judgmental and critical of others who are different from them. They are often unforgiving of behaviors and attitudes of others, forgetting that every person was created by God and that He loves them. Some people are incapable of loving because not only have they not experienced God's love, they may never have experienced love from another human being. They have been hurt by someone who should have shown them love. They think they are not lovable themselves or even worthy of love. Finally, there are those that believe you have to like another person to be able to love them. That's not true.

You can show love without necessarily liking another person. In one of his letters, John writes, "whoever does not love, does not know God, because God is love" (1 John 4:8).

Q11 HOW DOES GOD TEACH US TO LOVE OTHERS?

God teaches us by studying his word, by seeking his will, by listening to the Holy Spirit, and by observing the example of Christ. God's desire is for all people to put their faith and trust in Jesus Christ as Lord and see that they become more like Jesus. We learn from God by obeying his word and his commandments. Jesus said, "If you love me, keep my commands" (John 14:15).

The list of Jesus' commands is pretty short. They are easy to understand. Here are a few related to loving others:

- Love the Lord your God with all your heart, soul, strength and mind and love your neighbor as yourself;
- Honor the Sabbath and keep it holy and never take the Lord's name in vain;
- Share the gospel as you are going in your daily life. It's the "Great Commission";
- Be a good steward of your God-given gifts and of God's resources;
- Do those good works that God prepared especially for you even before the foundations of the world were laid;
- "concerning brotherly love you have no need that I should write to you, for you yourselves are taught by God to love one another" (1 Thessalonians 4:9).

CHAPTER 7

SIN, REDEMPTION, AND SALVATION

The three topics in this chapter are extremely important to examine as they are foundational for establishing an intimate personal relationship with God and Jesus Christ. Some of the most intriguing questions are raised about these three words; **sin, redemption** and **salvation**. The Bible clearly teaches that all have sinned and fallen short of God's standard of holiness (Romans 3:23). The consequence of sin is both physical and spiritual death. **Sin**, breaking God's laws, separates mankind from God. God, being holy, will not allow sin in his presence. However, God is relational and loving in character and has therefore provided a way to correct the sin and death problem. The word is **redemption**. It provides the only way to restore the broken relationship. God has been about the process of redeeming a sin-stained creation since Adam sinned and brought death upon all mankind and the ensuing chaos upon the earth itself. **Salvation**, the third subjective questions in this chapter, is dealt with in a direct fashion by answering seven critical questions. You will find the words "born-again" and "a new creation in Christ" being central to the main event of salvation. Enjoy moving along now in this adventure of discovering answers to more of life's greatest questions.

QUESTIONS ON SIN, REDEMPTION AND SALVATION

Q1 WHAT IS SIN?

Sin is any of the things we do, thoughts, words, or actions that displease God or break any of his laws or commandments. Among the things that displease God are ingratitude for his blessings, a critical spirit, a sharp tongue, a judgmental attitude, a hardened heart, a self-centered life, and an uncontrolled temper. Sin separates us from a relationship with God and with others. Unconfessed sin robs us of the joy of fellowship with our heavenly Father.

> "There are six things the Lord hates, seven that are detestable to him: haughty eyes, a lying tongue, hands that shed innocent blood, a heart that devises wicked schemes, feet that are quick to rush into evil, a false witness who pours out lies and a person who stirs up conflict in the community" (Proverbs 6:16-19).

The good news is that, if we confess our sins, God is faithful to forgive us and to restore a right intimate relationship with him (1 John 1:9). Only when we are walking in Christ's righteousness will we experience that peace of God that passes all human understanding. Life doesn't get any better than that except in heaven.

Q2 DOES SIN MATTER IF YOU ARE A GOOD PERSON?

Yes. Sin matters because it separates one from an intimate relationship with God. It is like adultery that destroys the trust between a husband and wife that leads to separation— emotional and often times physical. Sin also creates feelings of guilt and shame and can lead to depression or worse. The real question to consider is: by what standard or definition is a person "good"? The Bible says no matter how good or righteous we think we are, our righteousness is like filthy rags when measured against God's standard of holiness and perfection (Isaiah 64:6). So, it is clear by God's standard that you are a sinner even when you believe you are a good person. Therefore, if you are only a good person and do not believe in Jesus Christ as your Lord and Savior you will not be able to experience God's love and forgiveness.

The good news is that while we were yet sinners Christ died for us (Romans 5:8). Jesus paid the penalty for our sins on the cross. So now each of us can experience forgiveness and relief from sin when we put our trust and faith in God. That also means that when we stumble into sin again we can seek God's forgiveness and he will restore our relationship with him. When we abide in Christ and walk in the light of God's inspired word we are able to overcome sin and its power in our lives. Are you a follower of Jesus so you can enjoy God's forgiveness and the abundant and eternal life that is only available in him? If not, why not? What is holding you back?

Q3 WHAT DOES IT MEAN THAT THE WAGES OF SIN IS DEATH?

First, we need to remember that God is holy and will not have sin in any form in his presence. Basically, sin is disobedience. Breaking God's commandments and laws is sin. Jesus even went further; he said that hateful thoughts and the like are also sin. So, by these standards, all have sinned and fallen way short of

God's standard of perfection. Consequently, with sin came death to mankind. Death is the price to be paid; not just physical death, but spiritual death as well. In Hebrews 9:27 we read: "people are destined to die once, and after that to face judgment" There is no purgatory and there is no reincarnation. It is important to remember that death separates but does not annihilate. In other words, when a person's body dies, it is not over. In fact, the Bible describes three deaths as a result of man's sin.

Spiritual Death: This is the separation of man from God. It first happened in the garden of Eden when Adam disobeyed God's clear commandment to not eat from the fruit of the tree of the knowledge of good and evil (Genesis 3:1-7).

Physical Death: Adam's sin brought about natural death which separates the spirit and the soul from the body (Genesis 3:19).

Eternal Death: For the unsaved there is final death which separates man from the mercy of God forever. This eternal separation means that an individual will continue to exist but without hope and without ever experiencing God's love again. He or she is then condemned for all eternity; condemned to a place that Jesus described as utter darkness and weeping and gnashing of teeth; a place from which there is no hope of escape (Matthew 22:13). It is clear from God's word that death is certain and without faith in Christ it is the worst possible outcome a human being could ever experience.

Finally, one last thought on death to keep in mind. God sends no one to hell. Actually, people choose to go there when they reject God's loving offer of grace and salvation in Christ. The good news is that in Christ we have passed from death to life (John 5:24).

Q4 WHAT DOES IT MEAN TO HAVE YOUR SINS FORGIVEN?

To clearly answer this question it is first necessary to establish some definitional terms. Sin is an intentional or unintentional thought or act that separates us from our relationship with God or our oneness with God. It can be generally characterized as any serious failure in thought or deed that could have been avoided. At a minimum, it is a failure to live up to God's standards starting with but not limited to the Ten Commandments (Exodus 20). Our level of awareness or conscience helps us know when we have sinned. It is impossible to live without sinning. The Bible says:

> "all have sinned and fallen short of the glory of God" (Romans 3:23).

That is true because all humans have inherited a sin nature and being no longer perfect, they sin. The emotional, mental and physical burden of living one's life under sin is well-documented and keeps psychiatrists, psychologists and counsellors busy. Guilt, depression, anger, hate, broken relationships, greed and much more are all the result of sin. Fortunately, God's forgiveness will allow us to live without these burdens negatively consuming our lives. Forgiveness is both a once-in-a-lifetime experience at the moment of salvation and a continuous process for the rest of our lives. The good news of Christ Jesus is that he paid the price for our sins at the cross and now God's grace will redeem us. When we trust in Jesus as Lord and Savior, he will lift our burdens and make our lives purposeful and joyful (Romans 5:8). He shows us the love of God, and leads us to an acknowledgement of our wrong thinking or doing. He helps us confess that thought or act and request forgiveness and acceptance of God's grace. Then he helps us turn away from our sin and continue following Jesus. Millions upon millions of Christians have experienced God's grace and forgiveness and so can you. When you do this you will be able to move forward in your life at peace with God and reborn into the continuing newness of life in Christ. And, you will have fellowship with him now and forever. That's really good news.

Q5 HOW DOES A PERSON STOP SINNING?

Sin is sometimes described as missing the mark of God's best for us (James 4:17). We have all sinned (Romans 3:23). Even Paul, the great apostle who wrote a majority of the New Testament, reflects upon his struggles with sin in his letter to the church at Rome (Romans 7:19). Though Paul continued to sin, he knew that he could not save himself and that only Jesus could save him from his sinful nature (Romans 7:24,25). In his letter to the church in Galatia, Paul tells us that if we "walk by the [Holy] Spirit, we will not gratify the desires of the flesh" (Galatians 5:16). This will allow us to follow God's commandments as a testament to our love for him (John 14:15). Trust in God and allow him to keep you from sinning (James 4:7).

Q6 WHAT IS THE CHRISTIAN MEANING OF REDEMPTION? REDEEMED FROM WHAT?

First, it is best to consider the definition of **redemption**. It is the action of regaining possession of something in exchange for payment, or the clearing of debt. It also means deliverance from sin—being pardoned from the penalty of sin which is death and eternal separation from God. That's the answer to the "Redeemed from what?" question. Redemption, is a gift of grace by the creator, God, because sin is the rejection of God and his authority and only he can provide the remedy. Grace is the undeserved gift God has provided to overcome mankind's sin condition. That gift is Jesus Christ who took upon himself on the cross the penalty for all the sin that has ever been and will ever be. He paid the debt each person owes but cannot pay himself. In Romans 6:23 we read "The wages of sin is death (judgment)." That is why Jesus is referred to as Savior, as he alone has offered redemption or salvation to all who put their trust in him.

It is Jesus' death, resurrection and ascension into heaven that confirms he is the redeemer of men's souls. Sin seeks to keep men and women in bondage to the slavery of sin. Its goal is to deny them the freedom that God wants for every person—a personal, life-transforming relationship with Jesus Christ. Each of us was created to be in relationship with our creator and to experience a meaningful and purposeful life. We are designed to enjoy being in God's presence now and forever. The redeeming work of Jesus Christ brings abundant blessings and spiritual awareness to all who follow him. Remember, Wise men and women still seek him, how about you?

Q7 DOES KEEPING THE 10 COMMANDMENTS LEAD TO SALVATION AND ETERNAL LIFE?

If one could keep all the commandments perfectly their entire lifetime, you might think the answer could be yes. However, we learn in the Bible that no one is able to live by the law set forth by God. People try to keep the commandments and yes that is good. However, they break all of them regularly because all humans have inherited a sinful nature. It's in their DNA. God knew that people will not be able to live up to the law and he knew that the consequences of not doing so would lead to both physical and spiritual death. That's why in the time before Christ, God provided the Israelites with a way to atone for the nation's sins by offering a sacrificial lamb. In spite of this method for forgiveness of sins, the people continued to break the commandments, even worshiping idols, thereby breaking God's heart.

These Israelites were God's 'Chosen People' who, like people today, chose to be in rebellion against God. That's why God sent his son, Jesus, to atone for all the sins of the world, past, present and future. Jesus became the 'Lamb of God.' Jesus experienced death on a cross, to make it possible for us to have both abundant and eternal life. The only thing God asks is that we repent of our sinful ways, acknowledge that Jesus' death and resurrection are the substitute for our own spiritual death. In doing this, we are assured that we will move from death to life eternal.

Finally, why have people found it so impossible to keep the Ten Commandments? There are two fundamental reasons. One is man's sinful nature. The other is that God's standards of perfection are beyond man's capability. Just take a look at the Ten Commandments as listed in Exodus 20 to understand why it is impossible. The first commandment, "You shall have no other gods before me," sets the ultimate standard. We break this commandment all the time substituting things such as sports, professions, hobbies, personalities, etc. for God. Commandments two through five are equally impossible to keep. Now consider commandments six through ten, the "though shall nots": murder, commit adultery, steal, give false witness (lie), or covet. These are not any easier to keep than the first five. In fact, these are broken all the time too. For example, hateful thoughts, sex outside of marriage, half truths, using time at work for personal business or coveting what someone else has all break the commandments and are sins. The good news is that Jesus fulfilled the Law and placing your faith in him is all that you need now to be saved and have eternal life. Living by the commandments is still a good idea because God wants to keep you safe and from hurting others.

Q8 WHY WAS IT NECESSARY FOR GOD TO HAVE A PLAN OF SALVATION?

God, being omniscient, knew that it was a risk to endow man and woman with free will but he did. Rather than create robots, he wanted creatures with whom he could be in fellowship. He made them in his image with the ability to communicate and to show love. God knew they would one day these creatures would use their free will to make a bad decision and disobey. That decision brought both sin and death to God's perfect creation. Sin separates man from a holy God, but sin does not annihilate one's eternal soul. Therefore a plan for salvation and redemption was necessary. God knew that many would seek to renew a right relationship with him in love and would delight in gaining eternal life in the presence of God.

So, from the beginning, God planned a way for men and women to be forgiven of their sins, and to be saved from eternal separation from God. This is what is known as God's grace.

It was God's unconditional love that sent his son Jesus Christ, to earth to provide a way or plan for salvation. It was the way of the cross.

"For God so loved the world that he gave his one and only Son, that whoever believes in him shall not perish but have eternal life" (John 3:16).

In other words, the way of the cross is open to anyone and everyone who confesses Jesus as savior and lord. It is also the only way to God. There is no 'path' to God. It is that trust in God and his promise in Jesus that defines a Christian and the reason salvation was necessary. The important question is, "Have you trusted your life to Jesus?" The answer has eternal consequences. Heaven or hell is in the balance. Choose wisely.

Q9 WHY DID JESUS HAVE TO DIE, COULDN'T GOD JUST FIX THINGS?

These are important questions and the answer might surprise you. They involve a matter critical to the Christian faith. The answer to the second question is also the answer to the first question. In life there are many authority figures that need

ANSWERS TO YOUR GREATEST QUESTIONS

to be honored and respected and obeyed; parents, teachers, officers of the law, Government authorities and the like. When a rule or law is broken there are consequences and justice must be served. God is the supreme judge and ultimate authority (sovereign) over the entire universe and everything in it. So when Adam sinned and disobeyed God, death was the penalty. That disobedience broke the intimate personal relationship God intended for mankind and himself. God's holiness and justice demand that sin and rebellion be punished. The only penalty or payment for sin is eternal death for the entire human race (Romans 6:23). God, who is eternal, holy, **omniscient** (all knowing), **omnipresent**, **omnipotent** (all powerful), just, and in control of his creation, did 'FIX' the sin problem that man, Adam and Eve, initially created.

The 'FIX' was to send his son, Jesus Christ, to pay the price for man's sins by his death on the cross (John 3:16). Jesus clearly understood his mission on earth was to proclaim the kingdom of God and to be a sacrifice for the sins of man. He knew it was God's will for him to die. Jesus willingly laid down his life as an atonement for sin. In other words, Jesus paid the price or the penalty for our sins to establish a way to restore a right relationship between God and his children. It's called God's **grace** or unmerited favor. The Bible says, "without the shedding of blood there is no forgiveness of sins"(Hebrews 9:22).

So it was Christ's sinless blood that was shed to provide for man's salvation and redemption and a new beginning with God in this life and in the life to come in heaven (Romans 4:7 & 8). Those who put their trust in Jesus as Savior and Lord are 'born again' and receive eternal life and have their sins forgiven. Jesus had to die to fulfill God's requirement for justice because of mankind's sin. The good news is that the God of all creation is also loving, merciful, and gracious. He fixed this problem with the most expensive and precious gift and way possible, with Jesus Christ his only son. So our sins are paid for, and we no longer have to die an eternal death. This is why Jesus had to die and how the all powerful God of creation FIXED the sin problem once and forever.

Q10 DO YOU THINK WE CAN EVER LOSE OUR SALVATION?

No. Jesus spelled this out quite clearly:

> "My sheep hear My voice, and I know them, and they follow Me. And I give them eternal life, and they shall never perish; neither shall anyone snatch them out of My hand. My Father, who has given them to Me, is greater than all; and no one is able to snatch them out of My Father's hand. I and My Father are one" (John 10:27-30).

Once we have acknowledged that we are sinners and have no way to earn our way into heaven, and have accepted Jesus' death as the substitute for the death we deserve, our hearts are changed. We repent of our sins and turn our minds and hearts to our Savior. We allow the Holy Spirit to guide our daily walk. Unfortunately, we don't become perfect and we may sometimes wonder if we might lose our salvation, but Jesus' promise leaves no room for "what ifs" or worry Try as we might once we've been saved, we can never do enough or be good enough to gain entrance into heaven. That matter has already been settled. When we are saved by Jesus Christ, our lives are forever changed; not because of something we have done or will do, beyond submitting to God and allowing him to make us more and more like Jesus. Paul reminded the Christians in Ephesus of a universal truth:

> "For it is by grace you have been saved, through faith—and this is not from yourselves, it is the gift of God—not by works, so that no one can boast" (Ephesians 2:8-9).

Q11 HOW DO I KNOW FOR CERTAIN I AM SAVED AND HAVE ETERNAL LIFE?

This is one of life's most important questions. God's Word as written in the Bible says:

> "If you declare with your mouth 'Jesus is Lord' and believe in your heart that God raised him from the dead, you will be saved. For it is with your heart that you believe and are justified, and it is with your mouth that you profess your faith and are saved" (Romans 10:9-10).

If you have done these two requirements, then you are saved and certain of your eternal life. That new life in Christ begins the second you confess you are a sinner in need of a savior and invite Jesus into your life as your personal savior and lord. This promise of God is sealed and guaranteed by the Holy Spirit. At that same instant God's spirit becomes part of your body, mind and soul. From that moment on you are a new creation in Christ, a child of God and a member of God's family.

Now for the practical evidence of that decision. Here are some questions for you to consider and answer. Do you tell others about Jesus and what He has done for you? (Your personal testimony) Do you read and live by the truth of the Bible, God's word? Besides just reading the Bible, do you study to discover God's plan for your life? Are you acquiring a Biblical worldview? Do you experience God disciplining you like a father teaches a son or daughter? Is your conscience and heart right with God? Do you fully trust and obey him? Do you reflect God's love in your relationship with others? Do you attend a Bible teaching church and enjoy worship and Christian fellowship? Do you feel forgiven of all your past sins? Do you pray regularly and continue to ask God for forgiveness when you do sin? If these things are true for you, then you can rest assured that you are really saved and are a Christian and can live in the joy of God's love now and forever and have a life full of meaning and purpose.

Q12 WHAT DOES IT MEAN TO BE BAPTIZED AND WHY IS IT IMPORTANT?

Baptism is an outward and visible sign of an inner change that has taken place when a person accepts Christ as Savior and Lord. It tells the world, usually in front of several or many witnesses, that a person is now a Christian and not ashamed of it (Luke 9:26). Baptism symbolizes dying to self and then rising to a new life in God in this present life and for life in eternity. It also means that a person has decided to follow Jesus and now there is no turning back to the old way of life.

In another sense, it reflects repentance and forgiveness and acceptance by God. In a symbolic way, the waters of baptism means having your sins washed away and being resurrected to newness of life in Christ. In other words, becoming a new creation in Christ (2 Corinthians 5:17). And receiving the Holy Spirit.

Jesus in the great commission said, "make disciples and baptize them" (Matthew 28:19). If Jesus thought it was important, so should we even if we don't fully understand the spiritual reason for it. Jesus set the example by being baptized by John the Baptist in the Jordan even though He was sinless and had no sins to be 'washed away' (Mark 1:9).

Baptism has a profound effect on a person's mindset about their faith commitment. It is a constant reminder of God's saving grace. Baptism is an event which is never forgotten. It creates a memory of a lifetime. The time, the place, the pastor, the friends, and the witnesses all come to mind when a person thinks about their baptism experience. That is why baptism should take place when a person is of an age to make the decision fully understanding what baptism means. It should not be done just as a ritual of the church or to qualify for church membership.

While it is true that baptism is not a prerequisite for one's salvation, it does put a 'Spiritual Seal' on it.

GOD
ANSWERS
ALL
PRAYERS

CHAPTER 8

PRAYER AND PRAYING

God is a relational creator by nature and cherishes conversations with his children. The first example was recorded in Genesis where we learn that before Adam sinned, he enjoyed daily fellowship with God. Today Christians have the privilege of praying or talking with God on a 24/7 basis. Better yet, Christians have an advocate with God, Jesus Christ, who intercedes on their behalf. In addition, the Holy Spirit helps in prayer when a person is unable to even utter appropriate words to express their deep need or anguish. In Philippians 4:6 we are encouraged not to be anxious about anything but in every situation, by prayer with thanksgiving, to present our requests to God. God promises to give us His peace, the peace that passes understanding and to guard our hearts and minds through Jesus Christ. God can be trusted because He is a promise keeper.

Then we have the record of Jesus often going off alone to pray to seek the Father's counsel, guidance and actual words to communicate to the disciples. Jesus also taught the disciples what we refer to as, the Lord's Prayer, and which is a perfect example of how to approach God. In John 17 we have a record of the marvelous prayer Jesus prayed for his disciples and for all believers of the ages yet to come. You will want to read it for yourself as if it was written to you. In this chapter you will gain several new insights on the subject of prayer and praying including the mystery of how God is able to hear and answer the seemingly infinite number of prayers that he receives every day. If you are looking for wisdom, God's will or his plan for your life, then this is a place to make these and other discoveries.

QUESTIONS ON PRAYER AND PRAYING

Q1 DOES PRAYER REALLY WORK OR DOES IT JUST MAKE US FEEL BETTER?

Yes, prayer really works. There are countless testimonies of God answering prayers. And yes, prayer can also make you feel better as you share your needs and concerns with God who loves you unconditionally in spite of your shortcomings. Sharing your burdens lightens the load of worry or guilt or anxiety and gives you both hope and a joyful spirit until the answer comes in God's perfect timing and in a way that is best. Remember, God always knows best because He is Sovereign. God's Word promises that He will answer our prayers when we pray in faith and believing. God's timing may not be instantaneous, but it is never late. Jesus taught the disciples to pray in the Lord's Prayer that God's will be done on earth as it is in heaven. Seeking God's will is a key component when you pray. Jesus promised,

"I will do whatever you ask in my name, so that the Father may be glorified in the Son" (John 14:13).

". . . whatever you ask for in prayer, believe that you have received it, and it will be yours" (Mark 11:24).

"If you believe, you will receive whatever you ask for in prayer" (Matthew 21:22).

The apostle Paul when writing to the Philippians said this about prayer;

"The Lord is near. Do not be anxious about anything, but in every situation, by prayer and petition, with thanksgiving, present your requests to God. And the peace of God, which transcends all understanding, will guard your hearts and your minds in Christ Jesus" (Philippians 4:6).

One of the chief purposes of prayer is to transform the heart of the person praying so that his or her heart will more closely resemble the heart of God and to be drawn near to him. Prayer is not so much about getting tangible results from God as it is an opportunity to get to know God more fully. In other words, prayer helps us better understand what God wants of each of us and it enables us to establish a lifelong relationship with him so that we can love others as he has loved us. Remember prayer is the key to the power for living the Christian life.

Q2 HOW DOES GOD HEAR AND ANSWER ALL THE PRAYERS HE GETS?

Unlike we humans, God is present everywhere all the time. His attributes are described as "all knowing"(omniscient), "all powerful"; (omnipotent), and "ever present" (omnipresent). In addition, God never sleeps or slumbers. There are no busy signals or voicemails when praying to God. Nowhere is God's omnipotence more clearly seen than in creation. The psalmist wrote about a God who determines the number of stars and calls in each by name (Psalm 147). Awesome! The Hubble telescope has discovered that the universe contains trillions upon trillions of stars in billions of galaxies, so listening to and answering the prayers of the more than seven billion people on earth cannot be a difficult task for the God of the Bible. Unfortunately a small percentage of people regularly converse with God on a regular basis.

Here is another way to think about the question. Today in our high-tech world tens of millions of people are simultaneously asking questions of Alexa or Siri or Google and they get nearly instantaneous answers. People could not imagine such a thing 50 years ago, but now this is common practice. So why couldn't God who created the universe do much, much more. Yes, God has no limits to hearing and answering all the prayers of those who diligently seek him, love him, know him, and trust him. The equally important question is," Are you spending enough time with God and listening for his answers?" Prayer needs to be a two-way conversation.

Q3 IS THERE A WAY TO PRAY BESIDES THE LORD'S PRAYER THAT JESUS TAUGHT HIS DISCIPLES?

There are many kinds of prayers and many ways of talking to God. We are reminded to pray unceasingly. We are also reminded to get away to a private place when we pray. That was Jesus' practice early in the morning. A guideline for praying is the acronym, "ACTS'; Adoration, Confession, Thanksgiving and Supplication. **Adoration** is praising God for who he is, what he has done and what he has promised. God is the awesome creator of everything in the universe and in heaven and on the Earth. He is the author and sustainer of all life and the only way to eternal life. He is worthy of our adoration. **Confession** is admitting we have sinned and seeking forgiveness for those sins and wrongdoings.

"If we confess our sins, he is faithful and just and will forgive us our sins, and purify us from all unrighteousness" (John 1:9).

Thanksgiving is telling God how grateful you are for all of God's blessings and promises, for his living word, the Bible, for Jesus' atoning sacrifice on the cross for you, for Christian friends, and for family, for the church and for our liberties and freedoms and much more. **Supplication** is presenting your needs and needs of others for God's consideration and response. Sometimes the answer is immediate, sometimes it's later and sometimes the answer doesn't seem to come during one's lifetime. But that doesn't mean we should stop praying. God is a good father and wants what is best for each of us. When we engage in conversation with him and learn to hear his voice, our supplication becomes less what we want and more of what God wants for us.

Remember that God is everywhere all the time, so talking with him can take place anytime. And like a conversation with a friend or text with a spouse, it can be as short as a few words. Some people refer to the one sentence prayers as ARROW prayers, sometimes spoken when one is in a panic situation or in significant immediate danger. But Arrow prayers can be a word of adoration, or confession, or thanksgiving. God delights in hearing from us so plan on praying often so you continuously connect your life also with God's love, goodness and wisdom.

Q4 HOW CAN YOU DISCOVER GOD'S WILL AND PLAN FOR YOUR LIFE?

God promises that he will reveal himself to those who diligently seek him. Finding God's will is not a one-time event, it is a lifetime experience. It requires a willing and receptive mind and heart and a desire to discover how to serve God and others over time. The best way to find God's will is to spend time reading and studying His word, the Bible. That along with prayer, talking to God, are the primary ways to discover God's will. This basically involves placing faith and trust in God and the Lord Jesus Christ, believing God has a plan and purpose for each life. Ultimately, it involves giving your life over to him and being transformed into his image, his character and his virtues (see Ephesians 1:5-12). Those who discover God's will live an exciting and purposeful life. Those that don't, just exist.

Q5 HOW CAN ONE ACQUIRE WISDOM FROM GOD?

First we must believe in God and trust in him before we can acquire wisdom from God. To know God, we must have a personal relationship with Jesus Christ and have accepted him as Lord and Savior. In the Bible, in Colossians 2:3 we are told that in Christ are hidden all the treasures of wisdom and knowledge. The primary source of God's wisdom is God's word as recorded in the Bible. The Bible contains instructions for our relationships with others and provides guidance for making many of life's decisions. This is the first place to go when seeking God's wisdom. The Bible is often referred to as the "operating manual for life" that is "best investigated before leaving earth." God instructs us in James 1:5-6 that if we lack wisdom we should ask God. The condition is that we must believe and not doubt. We need to be honest with ourselves and not be looking for answers that confirm what we want to do. We must be fully committed to obeying God. James 1:7 says that if we doubt God, we should not think that we will receive anything from him. When we pray for wisdom, we must be patient as we wait for an answer. God's timing for things is often different from ours. When we receive the answer, it cannot contradict anything in the Bible. This is why Bible study and prayer are so important for the believer. The books of Psalms, Proverbs and Ecclesiastes are called the wisdom books and we strongly urge you to study them over and over again. In them you will find those treasures of wisdom and knowledge.

For God so loved the world that He gave his one and only Son, that whoever believes in him shall not perish but have eternal life.

CHAPTER 9

THE BIBLE — THE GOOD NEWS

The Bible is the best-selling book of all time for a reason; actually for many reasons. First, it is the inspired word of God, the source of wisdom and truth and the revelation of God's plan for redemption and salvation. It contains God's promises and laws. It also reveals answers to mysteries that can be the focus of a lifetime of study. The Bible is the operational manual for life and is best investigated before leaving earth. It is the only prophetic book that is 100% accurate and totally reliable. As if that wasn't enough to entice every person to explore the treasures in the Bible on a daily basis, it contains the "good news" that God gave mankind a personal way to know him in Jesus Christ.

Written over a period of about 1600 years by over 40 authors, its pages are in complete harmony with accurate historical records of peoples and events with absolutely no contradictions. These facts make the Bible a miracle in its own right. It contains the record of Jesus' life and ministry with overwhelming evidence of his claim that he was God and was one with the Father. That's proven beyond a doubt in his resurrection and ascension back to heaven.

The Bible clearly states that Jesus is the only way to heaven and eternal life (John 14:6) and that way is opened to all who decide to put their faith and trust in him as Savior and Lord. That's really 'good news'! The questions answered in this chapter have been selected to clarify some of the challenges from critics and skeptics, many of whom have not bothered to read the Bible or investigate its truths. Would you like to know how the Bible contains Jesus' exact words given that the first Gospel was written more than 30 years after his resurrection? Find out by diving into this chapter. You will be surprised.

QUESTIONS ON THE BIBLE — GOD'S WORD

Q1 DOES THE BIBLE CLAIM TO BE THE INSPIRED WORD OF GOD?

Yes, the Bible does claim to be inspired and has shown itself to be so by the hundreds of predictions exactly fulfilled years and centuries after they were made. This is so because God knows the entire experience of the human race as if it has already happened. The apostle Timothy wrote,

> "All Scripture is God-breathed and is useful for teaching, rebuking, correcting and training in righteousness, so that the servant of God may be thoroughly equipped for every good work" (2 Timothy 3:16-17).

Translations, and there are many, make the best effort to capture the intent and context of the inspired original. Hermeneutics is the study of scripture. One must go to the original language as far as possible to get the authors' full intent, meaning, and purpose of that written. Context, that is who is writing it, when it was it written, to whom it was it written, and the circumstances surrounding the passage, are all relevant for gaining understanding and discovering the treasure of truth contained in the Bible.

It is important to remember, early languages, Hebrew in particular, had a limited vocabulary estimated at 4000 words or less compared to 400,000 in today's English. Hence, most original Hebrew text words had multiple meanings making context of the passage very important. Greek originals of the New Testament were more precise and therefore were more easily translated into modern English. Finally, the Bible is absolutely the inspired word of God and God purposely provided it the way he did. It makes one's study of it so much more exciting and fun. Every time one reads the Bible he or she discovers more truths and gains inspiration for living a meaningful and purposeful life. Some say that the word Bible is an acronym for the phrase "Best Investigated Before Leaving Earth." We urge you and everyone to diligently take time to read and study God's word. We encourage you to make it a daily habit. It's one you will never forget. It will lead you to Jesus who is the only way to heaven (John 14:6).

Q2 IS THE BIBLE A PROPHETIC BOOK?

Yes. But first we need to understand why. The Bible is a prophetic book because only God knows the future. How is that possible? It's possible because God exists outside of time and space. While it is hard for humans to grasp or get their mind around the idea that God already sees the entire future of human history, he does. The book of Genesis is about beginnings and the book of Revelation is about the endings of human history. In between there are many prophecies that have already been fulfilled. Here are a few:

- The destruction of the ancient city of Babylon 200 years in advance of the event (Isaiah 13:17-22).
- Jesus' birth in Bethlehem 700 years in advance (Micah 5:2).
- Destruction of Tyre, the heavily fortified center of on the Eastern Mediterranean coast, was foretold by Isaiah 400 years before it was besieged and taken by Alexander the Great in 332 BC (Isaiah 23).

- The manner of Jesus' death foretold 700 years before crucifixion as a form of capital punishment was established (Psalm 22).

There are many yet unfulfilled prophecies to come. There are more than 100 prophecies regarding Jesus' second coming. In addition, the Bible outlines a coming war between Israel and the combined armies of nations from the north and east of Israel (Ezekiel 38 and 39). It also contains descriptions of many end-times events (Ezekiel and Revelation). You can actually see this Ezekiel scenario slowly unfolding now by watching the nightly news. We trust this brief response convinces you that the Bible is a book of prophecy and then it can be fully trusted in its entirety because it is the inspired word of the living God of all creation.

Q3 HOW IS THE GOSPEL MESSAGE "GOOD NEWS"?

The word "gospel" means "good news." It's the good news about Jesus, good news that dates back to the creation of the world by God and the creation of man who was made in God's image. God intended that the man and woman he created, Adam and Eve, would live in perfect harmony with him—enjoying perfect fellowship and being obedient to his commands thereby allowing them to experience perfect joy. The problem is that man rebelled against God, breaking the fellowship and learning that what they thought would be freedom, turned into slavery to sin. That brought all the negative consequences that humans experience today. Those include pain, suffering, broken relationships, lack of peace and death. God who is perfect could not be in fellowship with imperfect humans. Their sins separated them forever from God and ensured that they would suffer throughout eternity for their continued rebellion from God.

Through Jesus, his son, God provided a way for men and women to be rescued from the consequences of their sin. God let Jesus take on the sin of all mankind—a substitute sacrifice that was acceptable to God. Jesus laid down his life that those who willingly accepted this substitutionary sacrifice might have their relationship to God restored. That brought with it the promise of eternal life free of the consequences of sin. That's the "good news". What does God expect us to do with this knowledge that Jesus died in our place so we can be saved from God's wrath against our sins? He expects us to accept the sacrifice of his son Jesus, turn away from our sin, and have faith that we will experience peace in this life and an eternity of contentment with him. Christmas is a celebration of this "good news",

> "Today in the town of David a Savior has been born to you; he is the Messiah, the Lord" (Luke 2:11).

The final question is, have you believed it and accepted Jesus as your Savior? It is the most important decision a person ever makes. Merry Christmas!

Q4 HOW COULD THE GOSPEL WRITERS QUOTE JESUS?

The Bible is the inspired word of God. That means, God directed the authors to write without error or contradictions, as some claim exist. Jesus said to his disciples in John 14:26, "the Holy Spirit, whom the Father will send in My name, will remind you of everything I have said to you. Everything! God keeps his promises. For the skeptic and nonbeliever, there is proof of another kind. In Jesus' day, it was mainly by oral tradition that information got passed along from one generation to the next. In the Jewish tradition, a rabbi or teacher, which is what Jesus was called by the religious establishment of the day, would have eight to 12 disciples. Those disciples or students would memorize the rabbis' teachings so that after he died his words could be passed along or taught to others. Therefore, it is most likely that Jesus' 12 disciples did much the same, as they were raised in that tradition too.

There are modern day examples of such memorizing capability. For example, Fanny Crosby, the greatest Christian hymn writer of all time, who penned more than 5000 hymns, became blind at age 6 weeks but by hearing her grandmother read the Bible to her every day, perfectly memorized the entire text of the first four books of the Bible and the four Gospels, Matthew, Mark, Luke, and John by the time she was 12. She drew from this vast memory of God's word to create her hymns and other Christian writings. The human mind has a great capacity to memorize incredible details. If she could do it, so could the disciples.

Finally, if you are searching for truth in this politically correct culture where tolerance is valued more than truth, then read Jesus' words in the New Testament. In John 14:6 Jesus said, "I am the Way, the Truth and the Life." Jesus is the embodiment of truth. And if by chance you want to actually hear God speak to you, read the Bible aloud. It is after all, God's inspired word. The Bible is the operating and safety manual for life. Study well and often. And, don't leave home without it.

Q5 DO SOME BIBLE REPORTS CONTRADICT OTHERS?

Many people have wondered about this and the short answer is no. There are many differently described and worded reports of the same event by several different individuals, but upon examination, there are no, absolutely no, contradictions. Many of the events such as the crucifixion, his appearances after his resurrection, his birth, etc., are very complex and involved many different people at different viewing points. The writers of all were eyewitnesses to each and had to know Jesus personally which was a requirement to be included in scripture. Hence, each was written from his own perspective. Just as witnesses today, say to a small event such as a car accident, each will report what they've seen quite differently. God promised that each writer would be filled with the Holy Spirit and be able to recall and write what Jesus said and did When each of the written descriptions are examined, they tie together for a perfect report on the entire event without any contradiction whatsoever. God's word is without error because God inspired it (2 Tim 3:16).

Q6 WHAT DOES IT MEAN WHEN THE BIBLE TALKS ABOUT BEING "HARD-HEARTED"?

It is easy to report what the Bible says about being "hard hearted" but we will find it challenging to understand what is meant by what is said. Most of the references about hard hearts are in the Old Testament. We are not to be hard hearted toward the poor, Pharaoh's heart was hardened and would not listen to Moses and a Proverb warns us that he who hardens his heart will fall into trouble. Ezekiel reports that God will remove our hearts of stone and give us hearts of flesh that will allow us to receive God's Spirit who will move us to follow God's decrees. Jesus told the Pharisees that it was because of the hardness of hearts that Moses wrote the law of divorce, Paul told the Romans that hard and impenitent hearts lead to storing up wrath and to the Ephesians he said that ignorance was due to the hardening of hearts. It seems that with hard hearts we fail to listen to God, remain in ignorance, fail to act on God's decrees resulting in storing up wrath for ourselves. But Ezekiel reminds us that God is willing to remove our hardened hearts and open up an alignment with God's intentions and plans for our lives.

For most of human history the heart was viewed as the place where all kinds of feelings were stored. Today we know that the heart referred to here is the 'seat' of one's personality and believed to reside in the eternal human soul along with the mind, conscience and free will. It is our minds that are receptive or non-receptive to God's guidance of our lives. Today we call that understanding neuroscience. Our brains have some "automatic" functions that help us to survive, but much of what controls our lives comes from the choices we make, our core values, our worldview and our lifestyle. The point of the Biblical references to "hard hearts" is that not only does God endow us with the freedom to be open to God's Spirit — God desires to connect with our minds to help us align with that Spirit. Closed minds and "hard hearts" are not open to receive God's spirit of truth. Paul anticipated neuroscience when he spoke about how we can have the mind of Christ in which we become new creations. When we see or feel "hard hearts", we should remember that they come from our minds when unaligned with the mind of Christ and that God offers a mind-changing Spirit to help us. Pursuing the attributes of goodness, kindness, godliness, openness, brotherly affection and love will keep the heart receptive to hearing God and not becoming "Hard Hearted."

Q7 IS THE BIBLICAL VIEW OF MARRIAGE OUTDATED?

According to the Bible, marriage was given as a gift of God at the time of creation (Genesis 1-3). The creator made humans in his own image, both male and female. God's stated intention still is that the two shall become one in a blessed partnership, to give birth and nurture to children. This is the blessed relationship for the family for the good of life on Earth. Without it, there would be no future generations of human beings capable of experiencing and sharing God's love and forming a moral society. So, we can say with confidence that never is the Biblical view of marriage outdated. Challenged yes, perhaps politically incorrect, but never passé. The glorious gift of sex symbolizes and sustains this intimate divine union. The sexual act for humans is intended only within the boundaries of marriage. Marriage is intended to be a life-long relationship, "Until death do us part," based on mutual trust, fidelity, and chastity. After giving the gift of marriage, the Lord stepped back and proclaimed, "It is very good."

God's beautiful dream of what marriage was meant to be has unfortunately been tainted by sin and our secular human updates such as divorce, adultery, slavery, spousal abuse, and more recently so-called "open marriage," same-sex unions, and sadly, broken homes with single parents. We can say with certainty that there will never be an acceptable substitute for a Biblical view of marriage. The gift of marriage as God intends is still evident all around us. Loving, healthy family life remains one of the best parts of our broken world. It is the fundamental nurturing institution of any nation. Is Biblical marriage outdated? Heaven forbid! Thankfully, no.

Q8 WHAT DOES THE BIBLE SAY ABOUT CONFLICT RESOLUTION?

This life is tough and the hardest things are relationships, especially when they aren't healthy. For the most part, we can control ourselves and our actions; we can't (or shouldn't) control others. People offend us and we will get hurt. There's no hiding from that. Sometimes, it's intentional and other times it's not; sometimes they aren't aware of how and when they have hurt us. The Bible tells us to forgive in all things, though sometimes, we need to confront the other person (in love) (Matthew 18:15-17). Ultimately, Jesus died for all of our sins. God's grace and mercy extends to all, and should be passed through you to others. He forgave us even before we even asked for forgiveness, and we will never deserve forgiveness, just as others might never deserve it, Jesus told us he would forgive our sins, as we forgive others (Matthew 6:14-15). It is a hard thing to do to forgive, but it is required to have true peace. God's Holy Spirit inside of believers enables us to forgive. Ask God for the power and wisdom to make the choice to forgive today, and allow him to align your feelings with your actions.

Q9 WHAT IS THE BIBLICAL CONCEPT OF JUSTIFICATION?

Justification is an important event that takes place when a person becomes a believer in Jesus Christ. It is what God does to put us in right standing with him. Unfortunately, justification is often misunderstood by well-meaning Christians who think that it is defined by the phrase "just as if I had never sinned." In other words, they assume when a person trusts or puts their faith in Jesus as Savior and Lord, then God sees them as being sinless. That idea or concept is not Biblically accurate. God always sees a person as they really are, a sinner in need of a savior. When an individual places his or her belief and trust in the finished work of Jesus on the cross, then God declares that person righteous.

Justification occurs only once! It is how a person achieves legal/adopted standing before God as sons/daughters. It is the act of God bringing individuals into a loving family relationship with him in the present and for all eternity. In fact, the really good news is that being justified by God makes us "kids of God's kingdom" and joint heirs with Christ. It doesn't get any better than that.

Q10 WHAT IS THE BIBLICAL CONCEPT OF SANCTIFICATION?

Sanctification is a very important concept or process to understand in the life of a Christian. Sanctification simply means "to be set apart" for God's exclusive possession as a reminder to us of God's redeeming grace made for our salvation. That gift of grace of course was the gift of his son

Jesus Christ who paid the price for our sins on the cross so that we could be forgiven and restored to a right relationship with God our creator. Sanctification is the ongoing process by which a person becomes holy in God's sight by yielding his or her life daily to Jesus. It is a lifelong experience for the believer. We are reminded over and over again in the Bible that God never leaves us as we were before we experienced salvation in Jesus Christ. It is in fact a lifelong pursuit guided by God's Holy Spirit and God's inspired word. Like an athlete training for a marathon, sanctification is an endeavor that takes discipline, time, sacrifice, commitment, faithfulness, and a desire to please and follow Jesus and bring honor and glory to God.

Finally, sanctification requires getting into God's word on a consistent basis, participating in Bible studies, having a regular quiet time with Jesus, joining others in worship services and storing God's word in one's heart by memorizing scripture. The goal of sanctification is to, over time, make a believer more and more like Jesus Christ (Romans 6:1-18). As that happens, others will see Christ in the believer opening opportunities for those others to hear about Jesus and God's love for them.

I am the Alpha and the Omega, the First and the Last, the Beginning and the End.

CHAPTER 10

END TIMES — THE PROPHECY

In 1882, European Jews, in large numbers began returning to the Promised Land after 1900 years of exile in the foreign lands. Many believe that this Zionist movement of return was the "Dry Bones" and the restoration of Israel as a nation foretold in Ezekiel 37. God gave Ezekiel that prophecy over 2,500 years ago. Christian's of every generation, especially since 1900, have been thinking that they could be living in the "end times". Once the nation of Israel was established on May 14, 1948, Old Testament prophecies seemed to be coming clearer.

Another prophecy concerning end times is in Revelation 11 where two witnesses are said to be seen throughout the world at one time. New technology that allows billions to witness live events worldwide make such a prophecy more plausible than at any time in history.

The Bible also tells us that in the "end times", scripture would be available in every tongue. Most people in the world today have access to parts or all of the Bible translated into their language, and the proliferation of cell service worldwide has allowed scripture to penetrate the far corners of the globe.

The questions answered in this chapter are related to "end-times" events but in no way make any predictions about Jesus' return for his church or the other events described in the book of Ezekiel, Daniel or Revelation. However, we can be wise observers of Jesus' predictions of the "end-times" conditions described in Matthew 24 and in the global trends in technology, culture and morality. Jesus' return is a certain event; we just don't know when. However, we need to be ready as it could happen at any moment. As you explore the seven questions in this chapter, we trust it will make you aware of the times we live in and that you will be certain of your eternal destiny and not have to experience God's wrath during the "end-times" tribulation period.

QUESTIONS ON END TIMES – PROPHECY

Q1 ARE WE LIVING IN THE 'END TIMES'?

Those interested in scripture prophecy and are perhaps troubled by terrorism and chaos in the world today would like to know the answer to this question. It has been asked repeatedly since Jesus' time. His disciples asked this of Jesus and He said that no one, including himself can know the date or time but God the Father, (Matthew 24:4 ff). Some additional passages are in 2 Thessalonians and 2 Peter 3:10 where the second coming of Jesus for us will be, ". . . like a thief in the night . . ." We also have in 1 Timothy 6:15, the appearance of the Lord ". . . which God will bring about in his own time . . ." Finally, we have in Revelation 22:7,12, and 20 where Jesus says he is coming soon. But, but, but, and this is very important and significant for us, He did give us in several passages the SIGNS that will precede his return and the subsequent events following. Let's look at two that summarize these very well.

"People will be lovers of themselves, lovers of money, boastful, proud, abusive, disobedient to their parents, ungrateful, unholy, without Love, unforgiving, slanderous, without self-control, brutal, not lovers of the good, treacherous, rash, conceited, lovers of pleasure rather than of God, having a form of godliness but denying its power" (2 Timothy 3:2-5).

"For the time will come when men will not put up with sound doctrine. Instead, to suit their own desires, they will gather around them a great number of teachers to say what their itching ears want to hear. They will turn their ears away from the truth and turn aside to myths" (2 Timothy 4:3-4).

One additional critical sign is the restoration of the nation of Israel on May 14th, 1948. After nearly two millennia of dispersion, the return to the promised land and creation of a state is a miracle and many believe a fulfillment of God's promise to Israel for the end of times. According to the Bible, this key event needs to be in place before Jesus returns for believing Christians.

So, yes we could be living in the "end times." What should that mean to you and me? Be ready, place your faith and trust in Jesus Christ and be alert and live that new life he has promised for you on this earth and for eternity.

Q2 WHAT IS THE RAPTURE EVENT ALL ABOUT?

The 'Rapture' event is mentioned very specifically and in much detail and is referenced in multiple passages in the Bible, including these:

> "According to the Lord's own word, we tell you that we who are still alive, who are left till the coming of the Lord, will certainly not precede those who have fallen asleep. For the Lord himself will come down from heaven, with a loud command, with the voice of the archangel and with the trumpet call of God, and the dead in Christ will rise first. After that, we who are still alive and are left will be caught up together with them in the clouds to meet the Lord in the air. And so shall we be with the Lord forever" (1 Thessalonians 4:15-17).

> "Listen, I tell you a mystery: We will not all sleep, but we will all be changed—in a flash, in the twinkling of

an eye, at the last trumpet. For the trumpet will sound, the dead will be raised imperishable, and we will be changed" (1 Corinthians 15:51-52).

These verses tell us that all who put their trust in Jesus, our Savior, not the rest of the world, will be 'caught up', and be changed suddenly and then be with the Lord. Also included are all the dead who have trusted in him. We don't know when this will be as God stated it is a 'Mystery'. What is vital for us to know is YES IT IS COMING, and YES IT WILL BE FOR REAL. Each of us must ask. "am I prepared?"

Q3 WHAT WILL IT BE LIKE ON EARTH THE MOMENT AFTER THE RAPTURE?

This question seems to arise more frequently now as the global culture and morality continue to deteriorate. It is also a timely question given that the nation of Israel celebrated its 70th anniversary of statehood on May 14, 2018. Most Bible scholars note that the last significant prophetic event needed to be in place before the **rapture** could occur was the founding, once again, of Israel as a nation after its 1800-year diaspora. So, the stage is set. Jesus said when asked by the apostles about this event,

> "But about that day or hour no one knows, not even the angels in heaven, nor the Son, but only the Father" (Matthew 24:36).

Jesus also said that it would come like a thief in the night or when it is least expected. This warning needs to be heeded. Now is the time to accept God's gift of redemption and forgiveness and eternal life, because no one would want to be left behind for what follows on earth immediately after the **rapture**.

Now to the question of what it will be like on earth for those left behind. Three little words describe it best: panic, chaos and mayhem with a great amount of fear thrown in for good measure. Accidents will occur on a scale never imagined or experienced before and with that millions upon millions will die. Just think planes in the air without pilots, cars without drivers, trains without engineers, etc. True believers in Jesus in every profession in place on the planet will disappear in an instant. Christian doctors, EMS crews, policemen, soldiers, and the like will no longer be there to provide care or protection.

Lastly, at that moment, the primary restraining forces of evil, the Holy Spirit and the Christian church will have departed planet earth. Just use your imagination as to what society will be like. Evil forces will be unchecked. With the Christians gone, the Antichrist will make his appearance as a false peacemaker and he will be embraced during the period known as the **tribulation**. For more of the story read the book of Revelation and just be sure that you know Jesus as your Savior so you won't have to experience any of this horror.

Q4 WHO ARE THE TWO WITNESSES MENTIONED IN REVELATION CHAPTER 11?

The short answer is the bible does not tell us who they will be. It's a mystery. Therefore, only God knows the answer. However, this does not stop many theologians and others, including us, from speculating. The one most common suggestion is that they will be Moses and Elijah, since they were present on the

Mount of Transfiguration with Jesus and the three disciples, Peter, James and John, (See Mark 9:2-4). The next most common speculation is that it will be Elijah and Enoch, as these two are the only two who did not experience physical earthly death. Others say they will be two new unknown individuals specially chosen by God. The honest answer is that we do not know whom they will be but we are certain that they will be real men. As to their purpose, it is to prophesy.

That verb, to prophesy, means two things: to declare the word of God and/or to declare what is going to occur in the future. Picture two Billy Graham types proclaiming the gospel. In addition, these two men will have supernatural powers, and their testimony to Israel, Jerusalem, and the world will be true and profound. Anyone who tries to harm them will themselves be reduced to ashes by fire from heaven. (See Revelation chapter 11 for the rest of the story.) This will occur during the tribulation. Probably during the first 3.5 years or 1260 days. Remember that all who believe in Christ will have been taken out previously. The interesting aspect of this prophecy is that the entire world will be able to witness these two men. One hundred years ago it was a mystery and thought impossible but today we have electronic communications to every corner of the world. And just remember that the Apostle John was given this vision over 1900 years ago, confirming once again that the Bible is the inspired word of God since God alone knows the future.

Q5 IS THE MOVE OF THE US EMBASSY TO JERUSALEM PROPHETIC? PART 1

After waiting over 20 years, it finally happened. To set the stage for answering this question, let us first review a few of the Bible's "end-time" events and then see if and how this embassy move the may tie in. According to many Bible scholars, we are now in the Church Age Period and the next event for those who have trusted in Jesus is what is termed the **rapture**. Jesus comes down from heaven in the air and takes all the dead believers and the living believers up with him. (See previous answers about the **rapture**) The nation of Israel signs a peace treaty with a person called the Antichrist. Israel relies on the treaty with the expectation of a world peace. This begins what is called the Seven Year Tribulation Period and although the effects of the rule of the Antichrist are worldwide, Israel is a focal point. After three and a half years into the Tribulation, the true nature of the Antichrist is revealed and he, along with a false prophet and Satan, attempts to destroy the nation of Israel. It is during the second half of the Tribulation Period when catastrophic and devastating events occur worldwide. This is God's wrath poured out on unbelieving nations. A remnant of Jews escape Israel and at the end of the seven years Jesus returns with believers and defeats the Antichrist and his cohorts in the final battle, Armageddon. Following this period, Jesus rules with his people on Earth for a thousand years, a time known as the Millennial Reign. The Bible also suggests that at the time King David, the king of Judah who rained a thousand years before Jesus, will return as regent to rule over Israel (Ezekiel 37:24). These will be exciting times.

Q6 IS THE MOVE OF THE US EMBASSY TO JERUSALEM PROPHETIC? PART 2

Let's start the response by looking at where we are today. First, we must explore five perspectives to get a better understanding of upcoming events before we will know the answer.

First From A Moral Perspective

America today, and also Europe, Australia, and even New Zealand are in a progressive state of moral decay. Biblical positions on abortion, homosexuality, marriage, and others are being disregarded by governments and peoples everywhere. And, it gets worse each year not better. The Bible actually prophetically describes these present conditions:

> "There will be terrible times in the last days. People will be lovers of themselves, lovers of money, boastful, proud, abusive, disobedient to their parents, ungrateful, unholy, without love, unforgiving, slanderous, without self-control, brutal, not lovers of the good, treacherous, rash, conceited, lovers of pleasure rather than lovers of God—having a form of godliness but denying its power" (2 Timothy 3:1–5).

> "For the time will come when people will not put up with sound doctrine. Instead, to suit their own desires, they will gather around them a great number of teachers to say what their itching ears want to hear. They will turn their ears away from the truth and turn aside to myths" (2 Timothy 4:3-4):

Today every one of these is being fulfilled. If you doubt it, just listen to the news.

Second From A Physical Perspective

Many believe that the establishment of Israel on May 14th, 1948 was a seminal event in world history. Now all the promises and words of prophecy regarding Israel can be literally fulfilled. Israel and its capital city of Jerusalem, are at the center of world problems with enemies surrounding it on all sides, just as predicted. In Ezekiel chapters 37-39 prophecy concerning Israel tells of enemies near and far that will gather to invade the nation. Could Russia, Iran, Turkey, Libya, and others be the nations described in the Bible?

Third From A Communication Perspective

The proliferation of smartphones and the 24/7 news cycle along with a host of other technologies, allows people in every nation throughout the entire world to see events as they occur. That provides one way of fulfilling Bible prophecy that all the world will see Jesus when He returns.

Fourth From A Current Events Perspective

Technology and powerful forces in the financial sector are laying the groundwork for a single international financial system and a single economic system, just as predicted in the Bible 2000 years ago. The era of a cashless world is not far away. Is this the technology that will be used during the reign of the Antichrist? Additionally, anti-Semitism is growing daily, fulfilling the prophecy that all nations will turn against Israel including even America once the rapture has occurred. Lastly,

Jerusalem is to become the world capital of all nations under the Antichrist. America recognizing it as Israel's capital and moving our embassy there may be significant. Watch as other nations follow. Every nation will want to have an Embassy in Jerusalem as it will surpass the influence of Washington DC, Beijing, and Moscow combined.

In Summary, The Bible has been correct for 3000 years and there is no reason to believe the remaining prophecies will not occur as stated. Caution is required however, as we cannot know the day or the hour of Christ's return. So do not attempt to predict one. We are just to be aware of the times and be prepared, as it could be at any moment.

Q7 WHAT IS THE MILLENNIAL REIGN OF CHRIST? WHEN IS IT?

To fully answer these questions, we must review the sequence of end time events as written about in the Bible and how they affect both believers and non-believers. Though Biblical scholars differ in their understanding of these complex issues, they agree in their understanding of the effects of these events on those who have accepted Jesus Christ as Lord and Savior. We are now in what is called the Church Age which began following Christ's crucifixion and resurrection and the subsequent arrival of the Holy Spirit at Pentecost. This Church Age will continue until what is called the **rapture**, when we believers and all deceased believers in Jesus Christ will be "taken up" from the Earth and be forever with Christ. As to when, it would appear we are getting closer and closer to this event.

As mentioned in 2 Timothy 3:1-7 and elsewhere in scripture, sin will abound and man will deny and even mock Christ at this time. Then a period of time known as the **tribulation** will begin and last for seven years. During this period, there will be massive devastation and loss of life and there will be a world leader known as the Antichrist sitting on a throne in Jerusalem. This scenario is described in the last book of the Bible, God's Revelation to John. Immediately following, a period known as the Millennium, i.e. 1000 years, will begin. It will be ruled by Christ and we as believers will be with him as leaders. There will be also present those Jews and others who accepted Jesus as Savior during the **tribulation**. This is generally referred to as the millennial reign of Christ. Following this period, comes the final judgement by Jesus described in Revelation. That ushers in the eternal dwelling for believers in the new heaven and eternal separation from God (hell) for the non-believers. While the exact sequence of the events are debated by Bible scholars, the important thing for you is to know where you will be when Christ returns?

WORLD
RELIGIONS

CHAPTER 11

CHRISTIANITY AND OTHER RELIGIONS

From the beginning of time, man has had an inner sense that there is a force greater than himself and that there might possibly be life beyond the grave. In the centuries before God called Abraham to trust and follow him, nations created religious structures, i.e. religions, in hopes to appease the gods and gain favors like abundant harvests and fertility. Today there are numerous major religions all claiming that they have a path to God. It seems obvious that they all can't be right.

Christianity is unique among all other religions in that it is based not on what a person does to gain favor of God, but what God has done to restore the broken relationship between man and God. Jesus left the perfection of heaven at the behest of God the Father, to become a man. In that role he went all the way to the cross to die in the place of sinful man, carrying all the sins of all men for all time past present and future, and then coming back from the dead to demonstrate his power over death. His life is the best documented of all notable figures of antiquity. His death and resurrection are historical facts. His disciples and more than 500 others witnessed his life after death during a 40-day span before he ascended into heaven, an event witnessed by the disciples.

The death and resurrection of Jesus Christ turned 11 uncertain disciples into a dozen courageous evangelists who turned the known world upside down with the message of Jesus, the Messiah. The word they proclaimed was that Jesus was the only way to God and eternal life (John 14:6). Except for the Apostle John, the others all died as martyrs rather than deny the truth about Jesus. No one willingly dies for a lie!

The Church of Christ, Christianity, brought the world out of the dark ages bringing the light and love of Christ to education and universities, healthcare and hospitals, compassion within adoption agencies, homes for unwed mothers, and for great advances in science, literature, art and music. Christianity was the driving force to end slavery, create great charities and so much more. In spite of the history of the truth of Christianity, many today still seek answers to life's greatest questions such as: Is it true? Is it relevant? Is it really the only way? In this chapter, we'll explore some of the answers. Remember, God promises to reveal himself and truth to those who diligently seek him.

QUESTIONS ON CHRISTIANITY AND OTHER RELIGIONS

Q1 HOW DO WE KNOW THAT CHRISTIANITY IS TRUE?

That depends on who is defining Christianity. Basic Christianity is the understanding that a person cannot do anything, including good works or good deeds, to win a place in heaven. Christianity alone teaches that forgiveness of individual sin and the promise of eternal life with God are gifts offered to an individual by God. To receive these gifts of both forgiveness and eternal life, one only has to accept the gift by faith in Jesus Christ as Lord and Savior. So the question becomes, is Jesus true? Is what he says about himself truthful? Jesus, the first century teacher, is documented in the Bible and by historians of that period, Josephus and Tacitus. His teachings are among the best preserved words from antiquity. His birth, life, teachings, miracles, death and resurrection were all prophesied more than 500 years before he was born. Only God, who exists beyond both time and space, could know the future.

Jesus' miracles demonstrated his divine power. In his three and a half years of ministry, thousands were healed of all sorts of diseases and these events had many witnesses to testify to their authenticity. His death and resurrection are documented historical facts. Jesus was seen by more than 500 people, including the eleven apostles, during the 40 days He stayed on Earth after his resurrection. Jesus' ascension back into heaven had many witnesses proving again He was the Son of God. In addition, there are thousands of verified reports of Jesus appearing to people throughout the world, even to Muslims, who are accepting in great numbers the truth of Jesus as the human manifestation of God. They are recognizing that Jesus is the only path to an eternal relationship with God, the creator of the universe—the only entity who can bring true peace to the human soul and to the world.

Throughout history, many people have tried to hijack Christianity, to use the religion to advance their personal agendas. They have distorted the teachings of Jesus. They have killed and bullied and destroyed in the name of Jesus. However, even a casual reading of the Bible clearly demonstrates that Christians are called to love their enemies, to serve the poor, care for widows and orphans, and to reflect the love of Jesus in all they do. They are called into a life of service on behalf of God, not because God demands it, but because they are so thankful for what he has already done for them. This is the truth of Christianity. By contrast, all other religious systems are either unverifiable or irrational, thereby disqualifying them as being true. For these reasons alone you can know for certain that Christianity is true, but the question is: Do you believe it? Every individual has the free will to receive God's gift of salvation or reject it and pursue his or her own self-centered life. Heaven and hell hang in the balance of this decision. All other religions propose a path to God that is based in part or in whole on an individual's ability. Unfortunately, the fact is these are all dead ends leading to eternal destruction. There is no other path. There is only the way of Jesus Christ because he is the truth and he is God (John 14:6).

Q2 ARE ALL RELIGIONS THE SAME?

No. Christianity alone provides the only coherent explanation for life on earth and for what happens to us when we die. As the notion that truth is relative and that one opinion is as valid as another continues to grow, more and more people seem to believe that all religions are the same. Many so-called religious leaders deny the authority of the Bible and proclaim that reality and truth are in the eye of the beholder. They reject the idea that there is an objective and absolute truth that supersedes all others. That is God's truth, clearly spelled out in the Bible (2 Timothy 3:16). Though many desire for everyone to coexist in peace by suggesting that all religions (and no religion at all) are equally valid positions, they don't understand that perfect peace with God once existed on earth but that peace was destroyed with the fall in the Garden of Eden. The restoration of that peace can only truly happen again once everyone is in agreement with the truth: that Jesus is the only way, the truth and the life (John 14:6). All people are created in God's image and are given free will, so we can choose to believe or not—a choice that has eternal consequences.

At one point in the future, when Jesus returns, we shall all come in agreement (Isaiah 45:23, Romans 14:11). Any other teaching that does not align with this truth is the source of division (1 Timothy 6:3-5) that keeps the world from achieving true peace (Romans 16:17). While it is God that reveals this truth to everyone, we, as Christians, are not to judge or condescend to anyone that is not in agreement (2 Timothy 2:24-25), but, in loving respect and gentleness, be ready to defend the hope that we have in Christ (1 Peter 3:15).

Q3 DON'T ALL RELIGIONS LEAD TO GOD?

The short answer is no, they don't. There is no path to God as other religions propose. The world's religions suggest that through self-sacrifice, good works and performing a variety of religious rites or rituals that a person can gain eternal life and know God. Jesus, who is fully God and fully man, Emmanuel, God with us, said:

> "I am the way, and the truth and the life. No one comes to the Father (God) except through me" (John 14:6).

Jesus is also the source of all truth, so what he said can be trusted.

The only way to a present and eternal relationship with God is to commit one's life to Jesus as Savior and Lord, follow him and obey his Commandments. He said,

> "'Love the Lord your God with all your heart and with all your soul and with all your mind.' This is the first and greatest commandment. And the second is like it: 'Love your neighbor as yourself.' "All the Law and the Prophets hang on these two commandments" (Matthew 22:36-40).

He also said,

> "Go and make disciples of all nations'" (Matthew 28:19).

Salvation is a gift from God, not something to be earned by human acts. The apostle Paul wrote: "If you declare with your mouth, 'Jesus Christ is Lord.' and believe in your heart that God has raised him from the dead, you will be saved. For it is with your heart that you believe and are justified, and it is with your mouth that you profess your faith and are saved" (Romans 10:9-10).

This is the only way to God and to eternal life.

Religion can make people think that they are better than others because they are 'religious' and self-righteous. Jesus called out the Pharisees for their hypocrisy because they had the outward appearance of being religious but their hearts were far from God. They trusted in the religion of the law. However it only pointed out their sinfulness and hard-heartedness and was never intended to lead anyone to salvation. Christianity is the only way that leads to God.

Q4 ISN'T EVERYONE CREATED BY GOD A 'CHILD OF GOD'?

In this era of political correctness and so-called religious tolerance we are led to believe that all religions lead to God and we often hear it said "we are all children of God." Unfortunately, this is not true. It is completely correct to say "we are all loved by God." God created us in his image from before time began (Genesis 1:26). He formed us "fearfully and wonderfully" in our mothers' wombs, and knew us before we were born (Psalm 139). And, he loves us with an unconditional, everlasting love. It is quite humbling to realize that we can do absolutely nothing to make God love us more than He does now, and also there's absolutely nothing we do that will make him love us less. However, the Bible is very clear on this:

> "Everyone who believes that Jesus is the Christ is born
> of God, and everyone who loves the father loves his
> child as well" (1 John 5:1).

They are actually "born again" into God's family, with God as their father. Trusting in Jesus is the only way for this to happen. When you are born anew, you are loved as a precious child by the most loving and perfect father who created us and knows us completely and will provide, protect and guide us. Not only this, but since you are God's child, a member of the royal household, you are also an heir to God's eternal kingdom with all its rights and privileges. You are a child of the King — known, loved, gifted and cared for — now and forever. Isn't it wonderful to be able to relax and trust that all is well, regardless of what you see, because you know your Father is taking care of you? If you do not have that peace, you can have it today. Surrender your life to Jesus, and become a child of God.

Q5 IS THE GOD OF ISLAM THE SAME AS THE GOD OF CHRISTIANITY?

NO, the god of Islam is not the same as the God of Christianity and the Bible. In Christianity God is Trinity, (God comprised of three distinct persons: Father, Son and Holy Spirit) but in Islam god is not Trinity (God is one). It is impossible for God to be Trinity and not Trinity at the same time. Furthermore, because Islam denies the Trinity, Muslims reject the Christian view that Jesus is God. There is an inscription on the Dome of the Rock mosque in Jerusalem that specifically says, God has no Son. In the Quran, the holy book of Islam, in Surah 5:73 (Yusuf Ali), it is written, "They do blaspheme who say: Allah is one of three in a Trinity: for there is no god except One Allah." So it is clear that the Quran clearly denies one of the essential Christian doctrines about God's nature. The god of Islam and the God of Christianity are not the same. The god of Islam is characterized by submission whereas the God of Christianity is characterized by love. Also, in Islam, Jesus is not God in the flesh (Surah 4:172; 5:73: 9:30), where in Christianity he is (John 1:1,14). In Christianity Jesus was crucified, but in Islam he was not (Surah 4:158). In addition, Islam says that the "helper" is Muhammed, where the Bible says that the "helper" is the Holy Spirit (John 14:26). So, the god of Islam and the God of Christianity and the Bible are not the same. Muslims and Christians therefore do not worship the same God (Comments by Matt Slick).

Q6 WHAT IS THE DIFFERENCE BETWEEN AN ATHEIST AND AN AGNOSTIC?

These terms come up regularly in our secular world and it can be confusing to distinguish between them. An atheist says there is no God, while an agnostic says he doesn't know if God exists or not. In practice, atheists are "attack dogs" targeting all religions, but Christianity in particular. By contrast, agnostics are generally passive resistors. An atheist believes positively that there is no God, no supernatural, and that there is just life on this Earth and then nothing. In other words, when it's over, it is over. Hence, if God does not exist then there can be no divine or outside moral compass by which to live by. Atheists believe we humans are simply products of random chemical processes and natural selection, called the Evolutionary Theory, ET. Implications of this belief are far-reaching, because if one no longer has a divine purpose for living or behaving then all behavior is equally acceptable. Atheism is growing in popularity in America due to the influence of our liberal progressive culture and the aggressive tactics of organizations like the Freedom From Religion Foundation. ET is being taught at all levels of education, from elementary to college, and many bestsellers incorporate ET even though the theory continues to be discredited by modern science.

For Atheists, the effect of their disbelief in God is the elevation, in their own minds, of themselves as a god, setting their own standards of morality, hoping they will never have to account for their thoughts or behavior. As such, these men and women are not any better than the animals. They do not believe they are sinners in need of a savior. The joy of living in Christ is simply missing in their lives. They may experience times of temporary happiness, but never find joy or the true peace, grace and unconditional love that is only available through a personal relationship with Christ.

Agnostics say, "I'm not sure whether there is a God or not." Hence, agnostics are generally looking and searching and can sometimes be open to discussions on the subject of God and faith.

Q7 WHAT DOES IT MEAN TO BE A "NEW CREATION" IN CHRIST?

In the Apostle Paul's letter to Christians in Rome, he affirms that being a 'new creation' is rooted in a trusting faith in Jesus, the Christ ("God's Anointed One"). As new creations, God's character becomes explicit in our lives. Our values, priorities, and relationships are transformed. We gain a totally new frame of reference by which to live. Our view of God, our self-image, our sense of purpose, the direction in which we are aimed, the language we use, our openness to new exposure, the degree to which we perceive reality are all shaped by our frame of reference.

In that new creation frame of reference, doubt is displaced with faith, guilt with grace, hate with love, anxiety with courage, despair with hope, gloom with exuberance, and fate with destiny. And, we get a new moral compass, a spiritual GPS system.

In his letter to Christians at Philippi, Paul gave thanks for their partnership in the good news of Christ Jesus. He called attention to the importance of the humility Jesus modeled in his ministry and imploring them to have the same mindset as Christ (Philippians 2). Therefore, since we are new creatures in Christ, our habit of mental activity needs to be like that of Christ. Paul describes a divine power opening up God's new creations. Templeton Award winning, scientist, Holmes Rolston, provides a breathtaking narrative on how God prepared the way for you and me to have this mindset of Christ. He explains that our minds are designed to make choices. Our minds even seek a belief system to guide those choices. He says that in addition to matter, life, and mind, we find evidence of a fourth dimension that he labels Spirit. "Maybe," he adds, "our presence is embraced by another Presence." Christians identify this as the Holy Spirit of God. He adds," and this Presence "is eternal." When we are permeated with the mindset of Christ, we assume the nature of Christ and live in conformity with his way. When that happens, Biblical principles for living our lives will be natural gifts of what it means to be God's new creations.

Being a new creation means many things including: I am accepted, I am forgiven, I am loved, I am secure, I am significant, I am the salt of the Earth, I am the light of the world, I am a temple of the Holy Spirit, my mind is aligned with the mind of Christ, and I am a child of God. The Biblical message challenges us to be new creations. In Isaiah 40, we are reminded that: Those who wait for the LORD will gain new strength; they will mount up with wings like eagles, they will run and not get tired, they will walk and not become weary. In Ecclesiastes 3 and in Ezekiel 11, we read that God has set eternity in our hearts with a new heart and a new spirit. In Ephesians 4 we are told to put on the new self, created to be like God in true righteousness and holiness.

In the Gospel of John we are reminded that we shall partake of the fullness of the Christ as the branch partakes of the strength and vigor of the parent vine. When the mindset of Christ dwells within us, we have new eyes to see, new ears to hear, and new hands to work. Paul affirms that we can do all things through Christ who strengthens us (Philippians 4:13). We are "renewed" in knowledge and in the spirit of our minds. The "new Paul" who was created when the "old Paul" was crucified with Christ was a Paul who lived by faith that works through love.

Q8 IS CHRISTIANITY STILL RELEVANT IN OUR 21ST CENTURY CULTURE?

If you believe the recent PEW surveys, you might conclude that Christianity has become less relevant as our culture and technology have advanced and that Americas can get along fine without Christianity. Over 30% of American surveyed list their religious preference as none. That is a dramatic shift in the past 20 years. A closer look at the culture, however, reveals its moral decline, increased violence, higher divorce rate, and more self-centeredness than ever in America. When faith in God, in truth, and in Jesus Christ, become less relevant to society and individuals, the results are predictable. Ignoring God's commands and moral standards has severe consequences for individuals and nations.

The historical facts are that Christianity was the primary moving force in creating our Western civilization. Many of the institutions that we take for granted today found their genesis in Christianity including colleges, universities, seminaries, medical schools, hospitals, orphanages, Boy Scouts, Girl Scouts, YMCA, YWCA and hundreds of charities. Christianity has been relevant through the centuries and still is very relevant today in our high-tech society. Why is this fact true today? It is true because human nature has never changed. Man, left to his own self-centered desires, is capable of considerable evil as evidenced by the hundreds of millions of innocent people killed in the past century and continuing in the 21st. The recent shocking news about selling body parts of aborted babies and even killing newborns is another symptom of how callous and barbaric a nation's culture can become when the God of Christianity is removed from the public square and its public institutions, including its government.

The only solution in stemming the moral and ethical slide of America's culture is Christianity. Only God through Jesus Christ can change the hearts and minds of men to enable them to engage in noble, moral and ethical behaviors that define the culture of the nation. The Christian faith is the only one that gives individuals and nations the assurance of God's love, grace, protection, blessings and presence. So yes, Christianity is very relevant in our 21st century. America's destiny hangs in the balance. America will lose God's blessings without it.

Q9 SHOULD CHRISTIANS TRY TO CONVERT THOSE OF OTHER RELIGIONS?

All Christians are called to go and make disciples of all nations (Matthew 28:19). But Christians do not actually convert others. Christians are called to be Jesus' ambassadors to the world bringing the Good News of the gospel that Jesus alone saves. God does all the convicting of sin and shows each individual the need for a Savior. God does the converting through his Holy Spirit.

The role of a Christian is to engage in conversations and share testimonies while loving and showing compassion to those who have no knowledge of God or have a distorted understanding. Christians are commanded to take the good news to all, including atheists who deny there is a creator (John 3:16). Christians do all this because they are instructed to do so in many passages of scripture and because they want to share God's love and that joy of knowing Jesus as Savior. They want every person to experience that new wonderful transformed and meaningful life Jesus gives now and forever to all who believe.

So, why would they not want to tell others about their new life and savior? Remember, Christians only tell others about Jesus, the gospel and how He died and rose again for each person. We are only his ambassadors. We go and tell just like the Apostle Andrew said to his brother Peter, "come and see. We have found the Messiah, Jesus." There is nothing greater than seeing a lost soul find Jesus as Savior. Now how about you?

If you are a Christian do you tell others about Jesus? Perhaps it's a family member or friend or colleague that needs to know him. We encourage you to be that Christian friend that shares the Good News and points them to Jesus just like Andrew did to Peter. Then watch in wonder as God does a marvelous transformation in that person's life. What happens really does surpass all human understanding but with God all things are possible (Matthew 19:26).

Q10 WHAT IS APOLOGETICS?

This question and topic generally refers to Christianity. The word apologetics is somewhat misleading and has nothing to do with apologizing in the modern sense of the word. Apologetics is building the case for explaining and defending the Christian faith. So, the straightforward answer is that apologetics defines, "What Christians Believe and Why Christians Believe It." 'What is Believed' includes knowledge about God, creation, nature, origins of man, sin, morality, stewardship, life's purpose, Jesus Christ, redemption, salvation, heaven, hell, the Christian church, the Bible, the Old Testament, history of nations, end times and eternity.

'Why Christians Believe It' is rooted in the understanding that the Bible is the inspired word of God and therefore totally reliable in the truth it contains. Christians trust the evidence that proves the Bible is historically correct, that it is the best documented of all ancient books and that it contains prophecy that is 100% accurate because only God could see the future of human history as if it is already completed. The Bible is a miracle in its own right as it was written over a period of

1600 years by 40 authors in complete harmony and without any contradictions. Christians trust and believe the evidence of both Biblical and secular records, (Josephus AD 75 & Tacitus AD 116), of the life, teaching, miracles, death by crucifixion, resurrection (witnessed by over 500 people) and ascension to heaven of Jesus Christ. They further believe the evidence of the dramatically transformed lives of Jesus' 11 closest disciples who boldly proclaimed the truth of the gospel and were martyred for their testimonies. The fact is that no one willingly dies or is martyred for what they know is a lie. Then there is the miraculous contribution of Christianity to Western Civilization; literature, art, science, music, mathematics, medicine, education, philosophy, law and much more. Finally, there is the witness and testimonies of the hundreds of millions of followers of Jesus Christ through the centuries. Why so many believers? The answer is because Jesus is the only way to eternal life and a transformed life full of meaning and purpose. He is 'The Way' to receive God's gifts of joy, love, peace, forgiveness, contentment, faith and eternal hope.

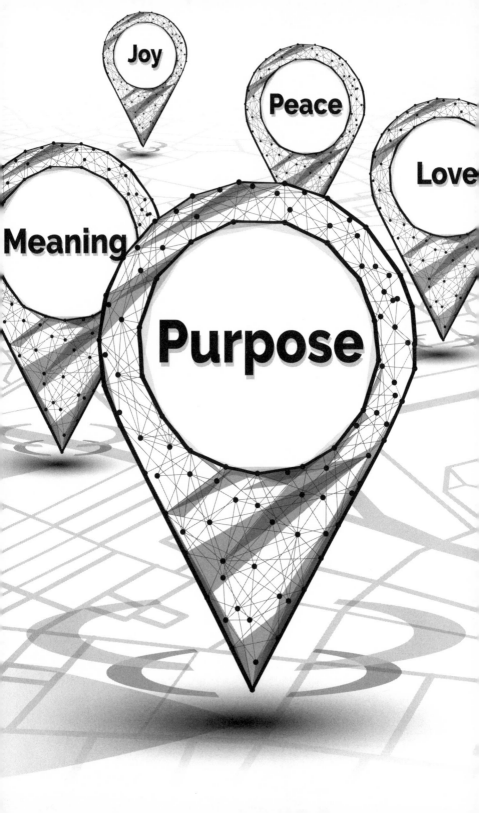

CHAPTER 12

GUIDE FOR CHRISTIAN LIVING

Living the Christian life can be challenging but is always rewarding. God has made becoming a Christian easy but as we have seen in previous chapters, living the Christian life is never easy. There will be times of great joy and times of tough trials. The good news is that God promises to be with the Christian through it all and guarantees that no matter what life brings, the best is yet to come. God also promises that he will never leave you or forsake you. When a person becomes a new creation in Christ he or she will experience numerous life changes.

The new Christian's worldview gradually changes from secular to Biblical. Interests change, activities change, attitudes change, relationships change, friends change, careers change and certainly life goals change. The point is that God never leaves a person like they were before they put their faith and trust in Jesus as Savior and Lord. God has big plans for Christians, plans that were actually in place even before the foundation of the world. Initially, however, God has to discipline, train, equip, test and spiritually enable the Christian to achieve all God has in store. This new adventure gives life meaning and purpose, peace and joy, and it honors God and Jesus Christ. In this final chapter and in the appendix that follows, you will continue to discover new information and more answers that will encourage you and guide you on your life's journey as a Christian.

Finally, and this is important, remember God loves you and wants you to know him through a personal, intimate and transformational relationship with Jesus. That choice is the most important decision any person ever makes. Eternity's destiny hangs in the balance. Now enjoy the final leg of your journey of discovery.

QUESTIONS ON A GUIDE FOR CHRISTIAN LIVING

Q1 HOW DOES ONE PREPARE FOR LIFE'S STAGES?

There are basically five stages of life; childhood, youth (teens), Young adults, middle age, retirement (golden years) and eternity. Each stage requires planning, preparing (education and learning), action (doing), learning from experiences, accepting constructive feedback. Ideally each stage should have a sense of purpose and meaningful achievement. Life becomes an exciting adventure at and through every stage of life when a person discovers God's plan for their life, trusts him to open doors of opportunity and proceeds in faith with a passion. The common element of all the stages is that they pass very quickly and then every person faces the reality of death and eternity. So, the single most important thing a person must consider is not planning for retirement, which is a good thing and should be thought through wisely, but where one will spend eternity. In other words, start and proceed with the end in mind. There are many resources available for planning and preparing for life stages. Some include Focus on the Family, retreats like the Walk to Emmaus, men's and women's Bible studies, BSF (Bible Study Fellowship), Christian conferences such as those conducted by FCA, Stonecroft, CBMC, Promise Keepers, and Beth Moore just to mention a few. The best resource for discovering God's plan, is studying the Bible, God's living word. Praying and having a personal daily life-transforming relationship with Jesus Christ will reveal your life calling and ministry for every stage of life.

Q2 WHAT LIFE CHANGES SHOULD A BORN-AGAIN CHRISTIAN EXPECT?

The short answer is that everything changes over time. The fact is that God never leaves you the same once you are born again. You will gradually know with confidence and certainty the truth. That truth is found in God's word, the Bible. Becoming a Christian doesn't mean that there won't be any trials or tests in your life journey. It does mean however that born again Christian has a new source of inner strength to persevere and build a strong character as a result of the trials. The source of that strength is God's Holy Spirit which comes within the heart and soul and mind of all born-again Christians the moment that they put their faith and trust in Jesus Christ as Savior and Lord.

So, here are some areas were change will definitely happen. Your mental state changes. Thoughts gradually move from commonplace to more in depth subjects. Interests become different from shallow discussions to concerned attentive conversations about what really matters in life. You might call these transformational conversations. Your relationship with family and others changes. There is the new possibility of real joy and understanding at home. You will experience closer and more meaningful relationships, more long-term relationships with friends where there is deep concern for each other's well-being. God's love becomes a real experience with your like-minded brothers and sisters in Christ. Your physical state will change. Over time, anxiety will be replaced with God's peace, since you will know with certainty your eternal destiny.

You will become more relaxed, confident and healthier because your interest will change from the trivial to things of lasting value. Your body has become the temple of the Holy

Spirit. You will want to keep it clean and healthy. Your worldview will change. You will look at the flawed world through the truth of God's word. You will be able to see secular ideas and values for what they really are, a pale imitation of God's design. You will be able to see through the false ideas by measuring them against God's truth. In other words, you will acquire a Biblical worldview. A Christian begins a transformational journey that never ends. Enjoy!

Q3 DOES BECOMING A CHRISTIAN MEAN MY LIFE WILL BE EASY?

Life is difficult. There is no way around that. We live in a fallen world where sin reigns mostly due to our human nature and our own choices, or the actions of others. Our own selfishness, pride and lack of trust in God often causes us to make bad decisions. God loves us so much that he gives us the freedom to make choices, which do have consequences. This started all the way back with the first man and woman, Adam and Eve. God advised them not to eat of a certain tree in the Garden of Eden, because he knew that they would die if they ate from it (Genesis 2:16-17). Satan, who was jealous of this couple and wanted to destroy their perfect relationship with God, got them to doubt God's word and disobey (Genesis 3:1-11). Their death was both spiritual—their relationship with God was broken—and physical—they grew old and died. Their disobedience created the broken relationship with God that all humans experience. But God wants to restore that relationship, and knew that the only way for that to happen was to have someone pay the penalty for our sins. That someone was God's son, Jesus, the only one who could destroy death itself. Many aspects of this mortal life will never be easier, and in some cases, become more difficult once we become a Christian. But, Jesus knew this and even told us to have peace knowing that he has overcome this world (John 16:33). James, Jesus' half-brother, also wrote that we should change our perspective when we face these difficulties, because they produce joy and maturity in us when we rely on God for help in these circumstances (James 1:2-4, 2 Corinthians 4:17). The joy of the Lord is our strength (Nem. 8:10).

Q4 WHY DO BAD THINGS HAPPEN TO CHRISTIANS?

His promise to every Christian is the same made to Joshua:

> "The Lord himself goes before you and will be with you; he will never leave you nor forsake you. Do not be afraid; do not be discouraged" (Deuteronomy 31:8).

God will never leave you or forsake you no matter what. That includes trials, pain, hurts . . . betrayals and anything else. Unfortunately, the reality is that evil exists and we live in a fallen world; a world that is stained by sin and by every person's natural sin nature. As a result, bad things happen and good people, even Christians, can get hurt emotionally or physically or even killed as a result. Many times life's trials drive us to cry out to God seeking answers. That is okay. However, remember God does not owe us answers. He wants us to trust him knowing that, in spite of our hurt, God loves us and cares for us. God often does allow suffering in this life so we can grow stronger, trust him more and often help others who are hurting. In this life we will often suffer from self-inflicted wounds because we have free will. There are consequences to choices in life for example:

Our bad decisions and mistakes

Going to the wrong places

Having a poor set of core values

Following the wrong examples

Listening to the wrong voices

Watching inappropriate movies and TV shows

Not knowing what God has said that could keep us
     from experiencing bad things

A person needs to know what the Bible says about God's rules for proper and meaningful living. The Bible is God's operations manual for life on earth. It is Best Inspected Before Leaving Earth. In other words, know its content well and don't leave home without it. Remember, your enemy, as a Christian, is the devil who wants you to doubt God and his word and not trust him. Also remember this. God loves you and will see you through your sufferings and trials. Trials will develop perseverance, which will develop your character and that character will lead to hope for the present world and the world to come (Romans 5:8, James 1:3). These qualities will, over time, lead to a strong mature faith in an all Sovereign, all Powerful and Loving God; a faith that will sustain you through life and into eternity.

Finally remember, Christ died for our sins while we were yet sinners to save us from the worst consequences imaginable, eternal damnation, eternal separation from God and eternal suffering in hell. That is how much God loves those who Trust in his son, Jesus Christ. It does not get any better than that.

Q5 WHAT IS CHRISTIAN STEWARDSHIP?

It's best to start this answer with a definition. A steward is a person responsible for managing another's property, especially a large estate. In the case of a Christian, a steward is responsible to God for managing wisely his or her time, talents and treasures in a manner that honors God and builds his kingdom, not theirs. There is no bigger estate than God's creation and kingdom. Now on to the question.

First, Stewardship is a personal matter between an individual Christian and God. The Bible is clear that each will give an accounting for his or her stewardship at the judgment seat of Christ. Second, stewardship is a voluntary choice not subject to the laws laid out in the Old Testament or the compulsion of New Testament church doctrine. Third, the Christian is to give cheerfully, graciously, abundantly and sacrificially, as he or she has been blessed by God. The parable of the talents and the story of the widow's two copper coin offering in Luke 21:1-4 are examples of God's expectations for stewardship of the resources he entrusted to individuals— invest wisely and give sacrificially. In 2 Corinthians 9:6 we are reminded to sow generously to reap abundantly. Fourth, stewardship reflects the condition of the individual's heart. A heart full of gratitude for all of God's provisions and blessings gives generously and joyfully. A heart that is not totally yielded to the Holy Spirit and hard-hearted and self-centered gives meagerly, if at all.

From a Biblical perspective, we find the first reference to the stewardship treasure principle of the tithe (or tenth) in Genesis 14:18-20 where Abram voluntarily gives a tithe to Melchizedek, King of Salem and high priest of the Lord God.

Ages before Moses and God's laws given to his chosen people, we read in Genesis 28:20-22 that Jacob promises God he will give a tenth of all he is given. Centuries later, Moses told the Israelites, to take a tenth of all the food and wine they produce into the presence of the Lord God (a designated place) and there eat it so that they would "learn to revere the Lord your God always." In another Old Testament passage, written almost 1000 years after Moses set forth God's law, we have an interesting reference to stewardship. In Malachi 3:10 God says, "Put Me to the test." God's promised reward for faithful tithing stewardship was an overflow of abundant blessings.

In the New Testament Jesus acknowledges the principle of tithing though he chastises those hypocrites who religiously follow the tithing law but neglect more important matters like justice, mercy and faithfulness (Matthew 23).

Today, the storehouse mentioned in Malachi and the temple where Jews brought their tithes, is now the church and it includes Christian ministries and missions. The priests of the Old Testament, the Levites, who received the tithe as compensation for their services are now our pastors, CE staff, missionaries and leaders of organizations like FCA, AIA, Young Life, Focus, Prison Fellowship, etc. As we can see, God has established a timeless treasure principle for stewardship and for supporting those who serve him on a full-time basis that is still valid for today. The Christian church could change the world if its members, true believers in Jesus Christ, gave at a level that exceeds the tithe and were faithful stewards of all God has entrusted to them—not only their monetary treasure, but their time and talents as well. Stewardship and tithing go hand-in-hand and are foundational principles of the Christian faith.

Q6 **WHAT IS TRUTH?**

Welcome to an elite group of thinkers, "the sages of the ages;" Aristotle, Socrates, Plato, and many other philosophers who have been seeking the answer to this very question. It wasn't until Jesus Christ came to Earth that it was answered clearly and directly. Jesus said, "I am the truth" (John 14:6). He is the embodiment of truth about all of creation and life's really important and significant matters; life and death, heaven and hell, sin and righteousness, creation and evolution, good and evil and so many more including all the little things in life. Webster defines truth as, "that which is true; that which conforms to fact or reality." Jesus' life is a fact and he is the ultimate reality. In order to know the truth one needs to know Jesus, not just know about him. A few of Jesus' profound truth statements for you to carefully consider are: "You must be born-again to gain eternal life" (John 3:3). "No one comes to the Father (heaven) except through me." (John 14:6) "The Father and I are one" (John 10:30). "I tell you the truth, before Abraham was born I Am" (John 8:58). In this statement Jesus confirmed he was God, (I Am), and eternal, i.e., he existed before Abraham in eternity past.)

Remember, truth is always truth. Two plus two is always four. In the same way Jesus' words are truth even though many choose to believe otherwise at their own peril. One final thought on truth. Every human being ever created that does not repent of their sins and accept Jesus Christ as Lord and Savior will face God on Judgment Day and no matter how good they have been on earth, they will be cast out of God's presence. That's a sobering truth that needs to be remembered and considered seriously. It's a truth that should be a life changer. The good news is that there is no condemnation for those who are in Christ Jesus. Examine the Gospel of John to discover more of Jesus' surprising truth statements. You won't be disappointed.

Q7 TRUTH VS TOLERANCE: DOES IT MATTER?

Tolerance once meant a free and open discussion in search for the truth. Modern science is based on searching for the truth. Tolerance used to be a respectful discourse open to "all points of view". In Western culture today it has become the god of liberal elitists and ultimately it leads to chaos and loss of freedoms. Denial of God's truth, as found in the Bible, the gold standard for morality and reason, results in the moral decline of society. That decline includes, but is not limited to, lying, fraud, failure to protect the sanctity of life, immorality, infidelity, disrespect for authority, selfishness, greed, and much more. Secular tolerance has become a new god where people offend no one and stand for nothing. The only thing they don't tolerate is Christian and Biblical truths.

So, does it matter? Yes indeed! If Christianity is not the truth, then the Christian faith does not matter. History suggests strongly that Christian faith and truth do matter. Western civilization is rooted in the Christian experience and worldview. When Christian truths are replaced by the god of tolerance, America, as we have known it, its virtues, values and freedoms, will no longer exist. Jesus said, "you will know the truth and the truth will make you free". Yes, Truth matters! Our democracy and our freedoms depend upon it. Never be afraid to defend the truth that makes you free.

Q8 ARE THERE ANY SECRETS FOR LIVING A PURPOSEFUL CHRISTIAN LIFE?

Generally speaking, most people want to live a life of meaning and purpose. But, there is no set formula for living a purposeful Christian life, because God endowed each individual with unique gifts and talents to be used according to his will and plan for each life. That said, there are actually some secrets that have been discovered over the centuries that have led believers in Christ to an exciting and meaningful Christian life.

A list of those secrets is presented in the Gems of Wisdom section of this book. As you embrace and live by these 10 secrets, be sure to keep in mind the scripture;

"Trust in the Lord with all your heart and lean not on your own understanding; in all your ways submit to him, and he will make your paths straight" (Proverbs 3:5,6).

In other words, when you put your trust in him, God will reveal to you an exciting plan for your life and all you need to do is embrace it and live it with a passion. Finally, remember our broken world needs Jesus. He loves you and wants you to share that Good News with everyone you meet! In Jesus you will find the truth you need to know for your life to be lived to the fullest and in harmony with God.

Q9 HOW CAN YOU SHARE YOUR CHRISTIAN FAITH WITH COURAGE AND WITHOUT FEAR?

Sharing your Christian faith involves risk and potential failure. Sometimes it may even be embarrassing. Yet there is an urgency about sharing your faith in Christ with those you care about because none of us knows if we will be alive tomorrow. Those who die without faith in Christ, are condemned to eternal separation from God in a place called hell. Remember, hell is every bit as real as heaven and is a terrible place to spend eternity. So, what are the choices about sharing the gospel message that Jesus saves and he alone offers eternal life to all who put their trust in him (John 14:6). One choice is to remain silent and allow that one you care about to try and find Jesus on his own. That is the coward's way and certainly not the way of a friend. The better choice is to muster up the courage to take the bold step of communicating the gospel message of Christ in a loving and considerate manner. Start with your story of what Jesus has done for you. Remember, success is not dependent upon you. You have been commissioned to do the sharing and God's Holy Spirit does the convicting and the saving. It's that easy. We don't save anybody but God does in his own way and in his time. To help you get a conversation going, we suggest you read and practice the principles laid out in *How Can I Share My Faith Without an Argument,* a free booklet in the Discover Series from Our Daily Bread Ministries (discoveryseries.org).

Finally, when you realize you just have to be faithful and that the outcome is in God's control the fear of failure is gone. God will give you the courage and the right words to share. The more often you share your story about how Jesus changed your life and the Gospel message the easier it will become. Just remember to pray, trust and act. The world needs Jesus more than anything else. It needs the Good News.

Q10 **HOW CAN I LEAVE A LEGACY AS A CHRISTIAN?**

Before we present the answer to this question, allow us to pose another for you to ponder. It may sound a little strange, but think about it for just a moment: what do you want people to say about you at your funeral? Do you want people to say that you were funny, or that you were financially successful? Do you want people to think you were generous or friendly, or a hard worker? Is that enough for you or do you want more? A legacy is about how we are remembered when we are gone. We all leave a legacy. It's simply a question of what it will be. In fact, you are building your legacy right now. When we die, our legacy lives on. A legacy may even last forever. The Bible says three things in life last forever: God (Deuteronomy 33:27, Psalm 100:5). The Word of God (Isaiah 40:8, Psalm 119:89). The souls of people (Daniel 12:2, John 3:16, Hebrews 9:27).

If you want to leave a legacy as a Christian, you must situate your life around these three eternal things. As a Christian you leave a legacy by investing your time, talent and treasure in God and in the things of God. You get to know him, love him, and serve him. You worship him regularly, and learn his ways. You do things that will give him glory. You give financially to his kingdom through churches, ministries and missionaries who are spreading his word. You listen to his Spirit as He guides and directs you throughout your life. As a Christian, you leave a legacy by knowing the Bible and speaking it to everyone all around you with your life, your words and your actions. You teach God's word to your kids, you share with your neighbor. God's word is your authority and source of hope in a lost and broken world. You study God's word to allow it to inform your life. As you do this, your character changes and you become more like Jesus.

As a Christian, you leave a legacy by investing in other people. People live forever, either with or without God. You share with others how they can know Jesus to ensure they will spend eternity with him. You disciple and mentor people, you love and serve and guide them. People and relationships are the most important thing to God. Jesus loved people and taught them, fed them, healed them and ultimately gave his life for that. At your funeral, what if instead of people saying that you were funny, they said, "here was a man who changed the world because he invested in eternity," or "here is a woman who invested in God, the word of God, and other people. She is someone who left a great legacy."

FINAL NOTE TO THE READERS

For additional copies of "Answers to Your Greatest Questions" and other books designed to lead you into a deeper relationship with Christ, please visit us online at *www.LifesBasicQuestions. com* where you are invited to leave a comment or a review. There, you will also find suggestions regarding how to use this book as a tool for evangelism, for new Christian growth and in a small group study.

You may also discover that "Answers to Your Greatest Questions" places you on a path destined to lead you and others into a better understanding of God's Holy Word. That is our prayer for you.

GEMS OF WISDOM

MESSIANIC PROPHECIES AND FULFILLMENT

For the Gospel writers, one of the main reasons for believing in Jesus was the way his life fulfilled the Old Testament prophecies about the Messiah. Following is a list of some of the main prophecies.

Prophecy	Old Testament Prophecy	New Testament Fulfillment
1. Messiah was to be born in Bethlehem	Micah 5:2	Matthew 2:1-6 Luke 2:1-20
2. Messiah was to be born of a virgin	Isaiah 7:14	Matthew 1:18-25 Luke 1:26-38
3. Messiah was to be a prophet like Moses	Deuteronomy 18:15, 18, 19	John 7:40
4. Messiah was to enter Jerusalem in triumph	Zachariah 9:9	Matthew 21:1-9 John 12:12-16
5. Messiah was to be rejected by his own people	Isaiah 53:1, 3 Psalm 118:22	Matthew 26:3, 4 John 12:37-43 Acts 4:1-12
6. Messiah was to be betrayed by one of his followers	Psalm 41:19	Matthew 26:14-16, 47-50 Luke 22:19-23
7. Messiah was to be tried and condemned	Isaiah 53:8	Luke 23:1-25 Matthew 27:1, 2
8. Messiah was to be silent before his accusers	Isaiah 53:7	Matthew 27:12-14 Mark 15:3-4 Luke 23:8-10

9. Messiah was to be struck and spat upon by his enemies	Isaiah 50:6	Matthew 26:67, 27:30 Mark 14:65
10. Messiah was to be mocked and taunted	Psalm 22:7,8	Matthew 27:39-44 Luke 23:11, 35
11. Messiah was to die by crucifixion	Psalm 22:14, 16, 17	Matthew 27:31 Mark 15:20, 25
12. Messiah was to suffer with criminals and pray for his enemies	Isaiah 53:12	Matthew 27:38 Mark 15:27, 28 Luke 23:32-34
13. Messiah was to be given vinegar and gall	Psalm 69:21	Matthew 27:34 John 19:28-30
14. Others were to cast lots for Messiah's garments	Psalm 22:18	Matthew 27:35 John 19:23, 24
15. Messiah's bones were not to be broken	Exodus 12:46	John 19:31-36
16. Messiah was to die as a sacrifice for sin	Isaiah 53:5, 6,8,10,11,12	John 1:29; 11:49-52 Acts 10:43; 13:38, 39
17. Messiah was to be raised from the dead	Psalm 16:10	Acts 2:22-32 Matthew 28:1-10
18. Messiah is now at God's right hand	Psalm 110:1	Mark 16:19 Luke 24:50, 51

Source: Prophecies of Jesus Fulfilled by Mary Fairchild, learnreligions.com

10 SECRETS TO AN EXCITING CHRISTIAN LIFE

- Honor God in everything you do: Life, Work & Time
- Trust and obey God always
- Have a daily quiet time with Jesus
- Enjoy God's presence, his Grace, Love and Peace
- Read and study the Bible and pray regularly
- Discover the wisdom found in Proverbs, Ecclesiastes and Psalms
- Forgive and forgive again and again
- Love, care for and fellowship with believers frequently
- Be humble and gentle, full of compassion
- Become a mature disciple of Jesus who shares God's Good News as you are going through life

Remember, most of all, that God is Sovereign. He can be completely trusted. He is in control. He wants you to know him. He Loves you. And, he has a wonderful plan for your life!

A PERSONAL MISSION STATEMENT

Developing and writing down a personal mission statement is an important exercise for every person. It is a very worthwhile investment of an individual's time in order to plan a meaningful and purposeful life that honors God and is aligned with his plan and will for life as a Christian. The first step is to spend time in prayer and asking God to shape your thinking on your personal mission statement. Next, take some time to listen for God's direction. Then begin to write down your ideas as an initial draft. These are the things to consider:

- What is my noble purpose and life calling?
- How will what I do honor God, build his kingdom, fulfill the great commission?
- How should I be sharing the gospel message of Jesus and be an ambassador of God's love and truth?

Secondly, determine what are your core values and guiding principles that will determine your actions and decisions. Core values are the filters which one relies upon for life choices and seeking truth. Some examples are: honesty, integrity (moral character), compassion, dependability, trustworthiness, kindness, patience, love, and forthrightness.. From the list, select six or seven that you will remember and treasure in your heart and mind and live by all your days.

Identify what will be your life's personal investments?

☐ Christian faith/ spiritual growth
☐ Family, spouse, children
☐ Physical and mental fitness
☐ Lifelong learning/Education
☐ Friends
☐ Good works
☐ A meaningful profession/ career
☐ Stewardship of God's resources
☐ Spiritual phone apps; ODB.org, AccordanceBible.com, BibleStudyTools.com

Determine how you will develop a spiritual life that leads to spiritual maturity, schedule a daily quiet time with God and enjoy and intimate frequent personal time with Jesus. Decide to pursue a Biblical worldview. (God's Truth vs. the Worlds' Opinions)

Finally, what are your goals and ambitions and dreams? How will you prepare yourself to handle life's trials and challenges? What are your hopes for the future? How will you make the world a better place? What kind of a legacy will you leave and how will you do it? How do you want to be remembered? A Personal Mission Statement will require fine-tuning as life moves along but the fundamentals remain the same: Love, Listen to, Obey and Follow Jesus and Trust God's Word and Promises.

LIFE'S BEST INVESTMENTS: YOUR PERSONAL ASSETS

FAITH
- Invest time daily with the Lord and in the Word.
- Be a faithful steward of time, talents and treasures.
- Fellowship regularly with believers.
- Share the gospel.
- Honor the Lord in all you do.
- Do good works God prepared just for you.
- Worship the Lord your God in spirit and in truth.

FAMILY
- Invest in time together.
- Create and cherish memories.
- Take plenty of pictures.
- Love, encourage, enjoy, protect, and support one another.

FRIENDS

Invest in building lasting and close relationships with a few personal and trustworthy friends, friends that will be there for you no matter what, friends that share your faith and core values and life interests.

REPUTATION

- Invest and live by a defined set of biblically based core values.
- Make your word your bond. Be a promise keeper.

EDUCATION

- Invest in life-long learning. Read a lot.
- Pray for wisdom. Find a mentor.
- Search for truth by asking discerning questions.
- Become a creative problem solver.

HEALTH

- Invest in your physical, mental and spiritual well-being.
- Eat right, exercise regularly, have a hobby, rest often, enjoy music, and laugh a lot.
- Cry in both joy and in sorrow; tears are healthy.
- Experience God's creation.
- Smile often as frowning makes wrinkles.
- Trust in the Lord always and seek His peace.

WORK

- Invest in your life calling.
- Work is necessary, desirable, fulfilling and rewarding.
- Work is God-ordained and should always honor him.

- Plan work time and schedules wisely. Don't become a workaholic. Write a personal mission statement.
- Become a servant leader enabling others to reach their potential.
- Respect the dignity and self-worth of every individual.
- Honor every form of honest labor, both mental and physical.
- Invest your gifts and talents wisely to build God's kingdom.

Finally, invest in leaving a legacy in family, in friends, in colleagues, in associates and in the community and in the nation. Be an American patriot and always walk in the path of righteousness with the Lord.

12 SCRIPTURES TO MEMORIZE

Philippians 4:13 *I can do all this through him who gives me strength.*

Matthew 19:26 . . . *with God all things are possible.*

Psalm 51:10 *Create in me a pure heart, O God, and renew a steadfast spirit within me.*

Proverbs 3:5-6 *Trust in the Lord with all your heart and lean not on your own understanding. In all your ways submit to him and he will make your paths straight.*

Mark 8:36 *What good is it for someone to gain the whole world and lose his own soul. Or what can anyone give in exchange for his soul?*

John 14:6 *Jesus answered, "I am the way, and the truth and the life. No one comes to the Father except through me."*

John 1:14 *The Word became flesh and made His dwelling among us. We have seen His glory, the glory of the one and only son, who came from the Father, full of grace and truth.*

Romans 1:16 *I am not ashamed of the gospel because it is the power of God that brings salvation to everyone who believes . . .*

Romans 10:9-10 *If you declare with your mouth, "Jesus is Lord," and believe in your heart that God raised him from the dead, you will be saved. For it is with your heart that you believe and are justified, and it is with your mouth you confess and are saved.*

Jeremiah 29:11 *"For I know the plans I have for you," declares the Lord, "plans to prosper you and not to harm you, plans to give you hope and a future."*

Malachi 3:10 *"Bring the whole tithe into the storehouse, that there may be food in my house. Test me in this," says the Lord Almighty, "and see if I will not open the floodgates of heaven and pour out so much blessing that there will not be room enough to store it."* Note: This is about stewardship. The Storehouse is the Church. The tithe is 10°/o of all income! Not to tithe is to rob God.

Proverbs 1:7 *The fear of the Lord is the beginning of all knowledge* . . . Note: Some day each person will be accountable to God for every deed done, every action taken and even every thought.

QUESTIONS FOR CHRISTIAN DIALOG

- Do you have any Spiritual Beliefs?
- That's curious. Where did you get that idea?
- Are there facts that support that view?
- How do you know those facts are true?
- Where is the evidence?
- What assumptions underlie that thought?
- What makes you think that's a good idea?
- Can you tell me some more about that?
- Can you give me an example that supports what you just said?
- I am not sure I understand what you said. Would you please repeat it again?
- That's interesting. Would you tell me some more about it?
- If what you believe is not true, would you want to know?

Jesus was a master at asking questions to direct conversations to discover the truth and to set out principles for life. That style of dialogue was the same used centuries before by Socrates and is even today referred to as the Socratic method. Asking discerning questions results in transformational conversations that can create opportunities to present the gospel message and introduce a person to Jesus and a Biblical worldview.

The questions listed above are those that can be helpful in engaging in an effective dialogue. They are questions that also indicate that you are actively listening to the other person and genuinely interested in hearing and understanding their views, opinions and beliefs. Actually, most are those critical questions for conversations on all important topics including religion, politics, science, economics, and relationships. Remember, a compassionate Christian asks questions to draw out the other person and then engage them in seeking real truth.

It is important to listen actively but without judgment. There's truth in the saying: "people don't care how much you know until they know how much you care." In a faith conversation, don't force conclusions early but rather allow the other to draw their own conclusions. When the Holy Spirit leads a discussion to spiritual matters you can ask, "So how are you with Jesus?" There is a way to know him. Are you interested in hearing about that way? This question can open up a special opportunity to be able to share the gospel message, your story and the love of God with someone who is genuinely seeking answers to some of life's most searching questions. At some point in the conversation a good question would be, "Would you like to know him?" Your conversation partner may even be ready to pray to invite Jesus into his or her life as Lord and Savior. All that's left to do then is to lead them in prayer. On the other hand, there still may be more questions that need to be discussed before a decision for Christ can be made. If time runs out, it would be good to provide them with something like the *Answers to Life's Greatest Questions* booklet and then arrange for a follow-up conversation. What's really important is to listen more than talk.

MY FRIEND, BY D.J. HIGGINS

My friend, I stand in judgement now
And feel that you're to blame somehow
While on this Earth I walked with you day by day
And never did you point the way

You knew the Lord in truth and glory
But never did you tell the story
My knowledge then was very dim
You could have led me safe to him

Though we lived together here on Earth
You never told me of your second birth
And now I stand this day condemned
Because you failed to mention him

You taught me many things, that's true
I called you friend and trusted you
But now I learned, now it's too late
You could have kept me from this fate

We walked by day and talked by night
And yet you showed me not the light
You let me live, love and die
And all the while you knew I'd never live on high

Yes, I called you friend in life
And trusted you in joy and strife
Yet in coming to this end
I see you really weren't my friend

SEQUENCE OF PROPHETIC EVENTS

1. Rapture of the church (I Thes. 4:16-17; I Cor. 15:52-54)

2. IN HEAVEN: Judgement seat of Christ (Rom. 14:10; II Cor. 5:10; I Cor. 3:14-15)
   - Wedding of Christ and His bride, the church (Lk. 12:36; Rev. 19:78; 3:4-5; 6:9-11)

     Note the three stages of Eastern marriage customs:
     a. Betrothal. Marriage contract. I Cor. 11:12
     b. Processional. The groom with friends go to the bride's home, escorts her to his house. Matt. 25: 1-13
     c. Feast. Wedding supper with invited guests. Matt 26:2

   - In Ps. 45:14, the virgins FOLLOW the bride.

3. ON EARTH: Tribulation
   - Israel makes false covenant with the Beast and occupies her land in a false security (Dan. 9:27; Ezek. 38:8, 11)
   - Motivated by Satan and a desire for spoil, the King of the North invades Palestine (Ezek. 38:11; Joel 2:1-21; Isa. 10:12; 30:31-33; 31:8-9)
   - Beast breaks his covenant with Israel, moves into the land (Dan. 11:41-45-)
   - King of North destroyed on mountains of Israel (Ezek 39:1-4)
   - Land of Palestine occupied by armies of the Beast (Dan. 11:45)
   - A great coalition of nations takes place, forming one government under the Beast (Psalm 2:1-3; Rev. 13:7)
   - Kings of the East are brought in against the armies of the Beast (Rev. 16:12), apparently as a result of the dissolution of the government of Gog.

- When the nations of the Earth are gathered together around Jerusalem (Zech. 14: 1-3) and the valley of Jehoshaphat (Joel 3:2), the Lord returns to destroy all Gentile world powers so that He might rule the nations himself (Zech 12:1-9; 14:1-4; Jer. 25:27-33; Rev. 20:7-10; Isa. 33:1- 34:17; 63:1-6; 66:15-16)

4. The Revelation of Christ (II Thes. 1:7-10; Rev. 19:11-16; 20:1-3)
   - Gathering and judgment of the wicked (Isa. 11:4; Rev. 14:14-20; Matt. 13)
   - Chaining of Satan (Rev. 20:2-3)
   - Gathering of the righteous (Is. 11:12; 27:1)
   - Resurrection of Old Testament and Tribulation righteous dead (Dan 12; Rev. 6: 10-11)
   - Wedding feast

5. Establishment of kingdom (Rev. 10:4)

6. Millennium (1000 year reign of Christ on the earth) (Rev. 20:1-7; Isa. 11:1-11; 35:1-6)

7. Final revolt led by loosed Satan (Rev. 20:7-8)

8. Christ conquers with fire from heaven (Rev. 20:9)

9. Earth renovated by fire (II Pet. 3: 10-13)

10. Resurrection of all the wicked dead for the Great White Throne Judgment (Rev. 20:5, 11-15)
    - New Heaven and Earth (Rev. 21:1-5; Isa. 65:17; 66:22)

(Note: Sequence compiled by Dr. Stephen Lebar)

ACKNOWLEDGEMENTS

First, thanks to the many people who have read the six books in our Living Dialogue Series on Christian discipleship and to the countless others that have asked many searching and thought-provoking questions on life and faith matters since we first published our booklet, Answers to Life's Greatest Questions, in 2013. You have inspired and encouraged the writing of this book and challenged our Answers Team to respond to well over 150 profound Great New Questions. They all have my deepest gratitude for their Herculean efforts to respond promptly and with a worldview based on Biblical Truth.

Thanks to the pastors Dr. Daryl Donovan, Dr. Ed Vanderhey, Rev. Hu Auburn, Rev. Tom Walsh, Rev. Kevin Schafer, Dr. Stephen Lebar, Dr. Chris Scruggs and our Ministry resident theologian, Rev. Irving Stubbs for their insightful Biblical knowledge, teaching, preaching and responses to many of the really tough questions. Without their wise counsel and life experiences this book would not have been possible.

Thanks for the multitude of Answers contributions by the entire robust Answers Team including, John Mauer, Scott Sommer, Tom Petersburg, Larry Jarvis, Richard Kolovek, Brian Regrut, John Murtha, Livi, Russ and Nancy Cooley, Lee Southard, Bill and Nancy Wessling, Ron and Janet Windahl and

Harry Pollard all of whom were always ready to field a Great New Question.

A special thanks to Richard Kolovek and Dr. Lee Southard, PhD, Author of the recent book, *To Know With Certainty*, who willingly tackled the difficult questions on science, creation and intelligent design. It was a daunting task to separate opinions from fact-based scientific findings.

I deeply appreciated and benefited from the many discussions with Pierre Loizeaux, Bible scholar and teacher. His insights into the Scriptures help me fashion properly edited answers to inquiries about God and End Times including perspectives on heaven and hell. He also influenced and aided in developing my Biblical worldview. Our Answers Team approach to all of the questions in this book was, "What does God say and what does the Bible say", not "what do we think."

Of course a great debt of gratitude is due to my good friend Dirk Wierenga who has guided the design, publishing and marketing strategy of our book series and this one as well. He has also suggested the way to develop the graphic images which introduce each chapter and the best formatting style.

I appreciate an enormous creative contributions of Brian Regrut in managing our Life's Basic Questions and Living Dialog Ministries Websites, answering questions and in creating the amazing graphics for each Great New Question and response that has been posted there over the past five years. A picture really is worth 1000 words. Brian's are valued at many times that. Brian was the inspirational editor of the final manuscript.

Katrina Salokar, Greg Robertson, Amanda Mitrani and Bud Stephens from Paradise Creative Group of Sanibel, Florida have helped in communicating messages to seekers and curious

Acknowledgements

Christians through, graphic design, editing, proofing, social media and much more. Also Bud Stephens at Paradise provided editing and creative writing enhancements to the answers in chapter one.

Another special thanks to the design concepts of Frank Guthbrod who created the 'eye-catching' front cover and chapter header designs for the interior pages.

The tremendous challenge of proofreading for this book was the task of my most special person, my dearest wife of 56 years, Jean Marie, whose eye for detail and extensive experience of preparing legal documents resulted in what I believe is an error-free text. What a true blessing. Any typos for which I am famous are my fault.

Thanks also to my good friends Bill Pollard, Allen Hye and Roger Palms for their wise counsel and guidance on the structure of the manuscript and helpful suggestions to make it a better product. A special thanks of gratitude to Bill and Jean Bares for their generous underwriting of the book project.

Finally, and most importantly, thanks to my Lord and Savior Jesus Christ who was along beside me these past five years and our entire Answers Team as we labored over providing inspired answers for the, 'Great New Questions'. Jesus and the Holy Spirit guided our thoughts to prepare answers based on Biblical truths that would bring glory to God and be life-transforming for Christians and seekers alike. Amen!

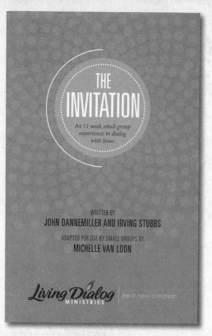

WOULD YOU LIKE TO HAVE A CONVERSATION WITH JESUS?

"THE INVITATION" is a small group study guide for an eleven session exercise designed to engage you in interaction with others by introducing in each session a new thought-provoking question relating to our faith in Christ. In group conversation you will be immersed in the truth of God's Word, answering questions as if you were having a conversation with Jesus.

This study is designed for groups of six to ten, creating an intimate, non-intimidating atmosphere in which you and your fellow seekers of truth will be comfortable, willing to freely venture comments, questions and answers. Jesus has given the invitation. Just come to Him.

Look for the other two small group study guides in our trilogy ~ The Transformation and The Way: The Christian Life. COMING SOON!

www.LivingDialog.com

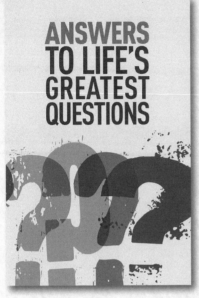

WELCOME TO THE LIVING DIALOG™ COLLECTION

YOU HAVE QUESTIONS - WE HAVE ANSWERS

If you have questions about your faith and the Bible you are not alone. In a world that embraces the idea that "truth is relative" knowing what you believe about your Christian faith is more important than ever. **THE LIVING DIALOG COLLECTION** consists of six books put together by a team of theologians using the Bible to address the greatest concerns of the Christian life. Each question is presented with a clear, concise, real-life answer. If you have questions regarding anything from Creation to Heaven, you can find answers here.

www.LivingDialog.com